HUNTS POINT

BY MICHAEL LUIS

Fairweather Publishing

Published by Fairweather Publishing

Medina, Washington

ISBN 978-0-9847882-0-0

Library of Congress control Number 2011942202

Design by Vivitiv, Seattle, Washington

For information or to obtain copies please contact:

Fairweather Publishing

P.O. Box 15

Medina, Washington 98039

425-453-5123

Cover photo: *Fourth of July at Hunts Point Clubhouse Landing, 1915. Courtesy of Town of Hunts Point.*

Inside cover photo: *Fourth of July at Hunts Point, 1915. Courtesy of Town of Hunts Point.*

Back cover photo: *Dock near end of Hunts Point on Cozy Cove, 1939. Courtesy of Washington State Archives.*

CONTENTS

LETTER FROM THE MAYOR   i

HUNTS POINT TODAY   1

HISTORY   13

ENJOYING LIFE IN HUNTS POINT   71

ABOUT THE AUTHOR   81

Town of
Serving Our Residents
Hunts Point

December 15, 2011

Dear Readers:

In 2005, The Town of Hunts Point marked its 50th Anniversary. During that summer, I interviewed all 32 residents and/or couples that had lived on Hunts Point for 30 years or more. Our goal was to write a book about the history of Hunts Point. Through several attempts with many volunteer writers, we produced a draft two years later.

Realizing how difficult it is to write a history book with volunteers, the Council hired Michael Luis to write this book, based on his recent success in writing the Medina history book. We are very proud to be distributing this book to all Hunts Point residents for Christmas 2011.

Those that contributed to prior drafts and pictures are:

Sarah Decker, Town Intern

Linda Longmire, Deputy Clerk

Sue Israel, Permit Coordinator

Cheryl Roth-Stein, Resident

Penny O'Byrne, Resident

Fred McConkey, Mayor

Kristina Surface, English Teacher

Dan Temkin, Clean Up Day Photographer

Ed Furia, Clean Up Day Photographer

Elaine Coles, Clean Up Day Photographer

We thank these people for the drafts and research which produced a steamer trunk full of scrapbooks, pictures, notes, videos, CD's, interviews, newspaper clippings, and biographies of the residents.

Since the Town cannot gift public funds, we took up a collection to publish this book so it can be given away as a gift to past, current, and future residents for Christmas.

The underwriting sponsors of this book are:

David and Sally Wright

Kevin and Krista Hughes

Rod and Janice Olson

Jeff and Korynne Wright

Peter and Molly Powell

Bruce and Jolene McCaw

Fred and Molly McConkey

Ted and Jeri Frantz

I'd also like to thank Town Staff members Jack McKenzie, Sue Ann Spense, Linda Longmire, Sue Israel, and Linda Kroner who contributed to the ongoing edits and production of this book. The true credit goes to Michael Luis, who took a box full of ideas, and created an accurate and interesting history of Hunts Point.

Ever since the beginning, Hunts Point has been a very special place. Its natural beauty is stunning, given its prime location between Seattle and Bellevue. Our town is a tight community of friends and families.

Overall, the families and the landscape do not change much over time. It is a great place to live, and we love it here.

Sincerely,

Fred McConkey

Fred McConkey
Mayor
1999 -

HUNTS POINT TODAY

Hunts Point, Washington, is a small community located on the east side of Lake Washington, tucked around the corner from Bellevue and within sight of Seattle's skyline. Residents here have something special: though they are close to major centers of commerce and industry, and can easily access the amenities offered by these large cities, Hunts Point remains a quiet, private town. People here sum it up best, stating with a smile, "We live in a park."

Hunts Point is small – tiny compared to its large neighboring cities, and encompassing only 205 acres (about a third of a square mile). Most of Hunts Point is set on a finger of land that reaches into Lake Washington, providing the majority of residents with waterfront property. The town remains faithful to the vision of its founders, with large, well-treed lots and no commercial enterprises. People come to Hunts Point because the sylvan beauty of the area calls to them, and they stay because they love the sense of community that makes this beautiful place home.

1996 aerial photo of Hunts Point, with Yarrow Point and Cozy Cove on the left, Fairweather Bay and Evergreen Point on the right. © Aerolist Photographers, Inc.

One of the four cities and towns that make up the Eastside's "Gold Coast" (the others being Clyde Hill, Medina and Yarrow Point), Hunts Point has attracted many prominent residents, from business leaders to well-known entertainers. Like all Hunts Point residents, they are attracted by the beauty of the setting, the lovely homes and the privacy afforded by the layout of the town. At the same time, the great majority of residents, both long-time and newly arrived, work hard to maintain a strong sense of community.

This balancing of privacy and neighborliness is a defining characteristic of Hunts Point. A drive down Hunts Point Road and a glance at the town's zoning map make it clear that residents prefer to live within the trees, out of view. But these same very private residents happily take turns on the Town Council and nearly everyone participates in the annual Clean Up Day.

Long-time residents who have seen the town evolve over the decades help to keep a steady hand on the tiller. "The minute I say we live in Hunts Point it seems as if we're living in a posh place, but it doesn't look that much different now than when we moved here in 1956," says

1937 aerial photo of Hunts Point. Courtesy of King County Department of Transportation.

1995 aerial photo of Hunts Point. Courtesy of Town of Hunts Point.

long-time resident Jeanne Bluechel. "Of course, then there was no bridge and there are a few more houses, but it still feels very much the same. The economy has changed, but these homes are very much lived in, loved and cared for."

LAYOUT OF THE TOWN

We can begin looking at the physical geography of Hunts Point from the air. The two aerial photos show Hunts Point in 1937 and again in 1995. The most notable difference is the addition of the Fairweather Yacht Basin, which changed the base of Fairweather Bay dramatically. Otherwise, Hunts Point has larger trees and more homes and docks and a large freeway, but few other major changes.

The finger of land that defines Hunts Point is the middle of the "Three Points" that were identified early in the area's history as noted geographic features. Evergreen Point, to the west, was its own distinct community before being included in the new city of Medina in 1955. To the east, Yarrow Point was the first to have permanent residents and became an incorporated town in 1959. Hunts Point is the longest of the three, stretching exactly one mile from the base of Fairweather basin, on the west, to the northern tip.

Two narrow bays flank the Point. Fairweather Bay lies between Hunts and Evergreen points. The head of Fairweather Bay was a marshy wetland when Lake Washington was lowered in 1917, but in 1957 it was dredged and filled to form the Fairweather Yacht Basin, adding 23 new waterfront home sites to Hunts Point. On the east side of the Point, Cozy Cove, originally known as Anderson Bay, lies between Hunts and Yarrow points. The base of Cozy Cove was similarly marshy, but the part closest to Hunts Point was filled and stabilized in the late 1970s, adding 20 new homes sites. The rest of the shoreline at the base of Cozy Cove belongs to the Wetherill Nature Preserve.

Once off the Point, the boundaries of the town appear somewhat strange: the city borders were drawn before the SR 520 freeway was cut through, resulting in some anomalies. Hunts Point's western boundary runs down the middle of 80th Avenue NE, which places both sides of the Fairweather Basin in Hunts Point. But once the new freeway was built, the homes on the west side of the basin were accessible only by driving through Medina. Similarly, the southern boundary was laid down the middle of NE 28th Street. But with the new freeway, this made five Hunts Point homes also accessible only through Medina. Several other Hunts Point homes lie along Points Drive, to the east of 84th Avenue NE, and that cluster could be mistaken for part of Clyde Hill or Yarrow Point.

On the Point itself, almost all building lots past Hunts Point Circle occupy all the land from Hunts Point Road to the water. These parcels vary from 60 to 450 feet wide, and from less than an acre to 4.5 acres. This pattern was established very early, as the 1911 map on page 27 shows. In the late 1800s and early 1900s there would have been little market for the uplands of the Point, so no one thought to subdivide their parcels. The King County Assessor formalized the layout with an Assessor's Plat, and once the town incorporated, the full-length parcels became solidified in the zoning code. With recent lot consolidations there are now fewer homes on the Point than in the past and some noticeably larger lots.

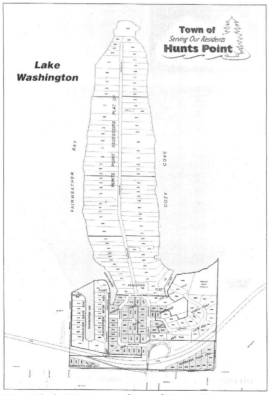

Hunts Point in 2011. Courtesy of Town of Hunts Point.

The areas south of the Point were laid out as formal subdivisions. The first was the Barnabee

Park Addition, platted in 1925, that included the homes in Hunts Point along Points Drive and extended into what are now Yarrow Point and Clyde Hill (much of Barnabee Park is in the SR 520 right of way). The area around Hunts Point Circle was laid out as a formal subdivision, Hunts Point Park Addition, in 1951. The Fairweather Yacht Basin was platted in 1956 and extended across the future SR 520 corridor to include those homes on NE 28th Street on the south side of the freeway. The final piece of today's town, the Hunts Point Lane Addition, was established as a formal subdivision in 1976.

The most conspicuous man-made feature of Hunts Point is the four-lane freeway that crosses the southern part of the town. As will be discussed later, the Montlake-Evergreen Point alignment was under discussion from the early 1950s and finalized in 1957, shortly after incorporation. Construction began in January, 1961 and the freeway opened in August, 1963. The current SR 520 freeway right-of-way encompasses about 20 acres of the town.

The only non-residential parts of the town consist of the Weatherill Nature Preserve, the Town Hall (originally the site of Bay School) and Hunts Point Park. There are no institutions or commercial enterprises on Hunts Point.

The map show Hunts Point as it exists today. Although most of the original homes have been replaced, little has changed about the physical layout of the town since the SR 520 corridor was built. And even less is likely to change once the new freeway expansion is completed.

WHO LIVES HERE?

The 2010 Census, shows a population of 394 people living in 151 occupied homes in the Town of Hunts Point. The census counts a total of 181 homes, leaving 30 vacant at the time the census was taken. Both the population and household count are lower than shown in the 1990 and 2000 census, primarily due to fewer houses: older properties have been combined into larger home sites. Homes have had about the same average number of people -- between 2.6 and 2.7 -- over the past 20 years.

Hunts Point has aged in the past decade, with the median age climbing from 45 to 50 years old. At the same time, though, children under 18 have continued to make up just over a quarter of the population, with 30 percent of households having at least one child under 18 at home. Hunts Point has experienced the same surge in young families that has been seen across Medina and the points communities as homes built in the 1950s and 1960s have turned over to the next generation of younger families.

HUNTS POINT IN THE REGION

The charm of small, suburban cities and towns is that they offer their residents the advantages of small town living, but with access to the economic and social activity of the larger region. Within the four-county metropolitan region centered on the Seattle-Tacoma-Everett axis, there are a total of 82 incorporated places, and 23 of those have populations smaller than 5,000. Hunts Point is on the smaller end of the size spectrum in the region, but five towns are even smaller.

In the history discussion that follows, we see that Hunts Point developed as a community along with other distinct areas of the central Eastside. Hunts Point, like Medina, was never a successful agricultural area. It served initially as a place for vacation cabins for the middle class and country estates for wealthy business people of Seattle, and gradually became a home for commuters. In other words, Hunts Point has always relied on economic activity elsewhere in the region to support its population.

That is certainly the case today. The points communities have seen a resurgence of younger families as the tech boom of the Eastside has created a new generation of successful younger people who have found in this area attractive neighborhoods, excellent schools and an easy commute to Redmond, Bellevue, Kirkland and other rapidly growing Eastside employment centers. And with a freeway onramp heading directly to Seattle, Hunts Point residents have a very easy commute to Seattle.

Hunts Point is similarly dependent on the surrounding region for shopping, commercial services and cultural activities. Residents of

Chicken coops like this one from the 1930s, located at 3226 Hunts Point Road, would be discouraged in the Town today. Courtesy of Washington State Archives.

the town have a short drive to downtown Bellevue, where shopping is abundant, and an easy drive to Seattle for even more retail opportunities, as well as regional entertainment and cultural centers.

When it was first settled, Hunts Point was quite a remote outpost of civilization, with residents needing to row themselves across the lake or flag down a steamer to get to paved roads and fresh bread. Today, Hunts Point and the other points communities are ideally situated in the very center of a growing and dynamic region.

GOVERNMENT AND PUBLIC SERVICES

When the points communities were considering incorporation in the mid-1950s, a number of voices, including the Municipal League of King County and the editor of the Bellevue American, urged these then-unincorporated areas to annex to Bellevue. In small local governments they saw only fragmentation and inefficiency. All four, of course, followed through with incorporation, as have small cities more recently, such as Newcastle.

It turns out that small cities are not inherently less efficient than large ones. In fact, per-house expenditures by the Town of Hunts Point are comparable to those in Bellevue. Although most residents could certainly afford more lavish local government, they enjoy excellent services at a moderate cost.

The key to this fiscal arrangement is the "Lakewood Plan," named after a city in the Los Angeles area that pioneered a new form of local government. As suburbs were growing in the 1950s residents of unincorporated areas sought a greater voice in their future, and that mostly meant having control over zoning, local transportation and other planning and land use matters. Indeed, the incorporation movements in both Hunts Point and Yarrow Point had their origins in proposals for high density residential development. Residents of the points also knew that a second Lake Washington bridge was on the drawing boards and that a Montlake-Evergreen Point route was a serious contender.

Promoters of incorporation realized they could create new towns and cities and gain control of their physical environment while, at the same time, avoiding the headaches of public administration by contracting with other governments or private firms for most government services. Hunts Point has taken the Lakewood Plan to the extreme, having only 1.5 town employees at any one time. All town services are provided under contract. Today, the City of Bellevue provides fire protection and emergency services, as well as water and sewer utilities. The City of Medina provides police protection and the City of Kirkland provides municipal court services. Planning and building services, street and park maintenance and other professional services are provided by private service and consulting firms under contract to the town.

Hunts Point's minimal government requires only a modest Town Hall. Courtesy of Town of Hunts Point.

Hunts Point residents also receive services directly from other governments. Hunts Point is covered by the Bellevue School District: children in the town attend Clyde Hill Elementary, Chinook Middle School and Bellevue High School. Hunts Point voters have, however, declined to annex to the King County Library District: library district taxes are based on assessed value and would average about $1,800 per year for Hunts Point homeowners.

In many ways, Hunts Point has perfected the art of minimalist government. A small, very private community does not generate demand for many of the services that larger municipalities must provide. But at the same time, Hunts Point has no commercial tax base at all. Hunts Point generates half of its revenue from property taxes and the balance from building permits when properties are built and excise taxes on the sale of homes. The vast majority of the local sales taxes paid by residents ends up in the coffers of Bellevue, Seattle and other commercial centers. But the beauty of our fragmented system of local government is that communities have choices about what type of government they want, and Hunts Point residents have chosen to keep it very simple.

GOVERNING WITH A LIGHT TOUCH

The simplicity of Hunts Point government is matched by the prevalent leadership style in the town. The trend has been for mayors and town staff to remain in office for a long time, while councilmembers often stay for two or three terms, adding stability to town decisions.

Hunts Point was incorporated as a "town", under Washington State law, which defines a town as having fewer than 1,500 residents at the time of incorporation. Unlike larger cities that generally have a council-manager form of government, towns elect both a mayor and a five-member town council, with the mayor having executive authority. The mayor appoints a town administrator and

Mayor Fred McConkey, far left, speaks to Town Councilmembers in 2005. Left to right: Ted Frantz, Jeri Boettcher, Jim Nordstrom, Jeff Wright (Jan Brekke not pictured). Courtesy of Town of Hunts Point.

other staff as needed, and is responsible for the day-to-day conduct of the town's business. Towns can choose to adopt a council-manager government, such as Medina's, but Hunts Point has stayed with the original form prescribed by the state.

CHALLENGE FOR THE FUTURE: PRIVACY AND SAFETY WITHOUT GATES

The individuals and families that make up much of Hunts Point's population may have choosen to live in secure, gated communities to help ensure their privacy and safety. These are real concerns and it is hard to fault people for wanting strict control of their surroundings. But Hunts Point is different in this respect.

Although the number of households in Hunts Point is similar to that of Seattle's gated Broadmoor and Highlands communities, Hunts Point remains open to all visitors. Hunts Point Road, a dead end with sparse traffic, is a lovely place for a walk or a bike ride, and people from around the region can be seen enjoying the ambience. But so far, this openness has not raised enough concerns for the town to restrict access.

And most residents want it this way. A residential island is a different place than a town that is open to all. The installation of security cameras at the entrance to Hunts Point has sharply reduced crime in

The single entrance to Hunts Point is marked by this traffic circle. Courtesy of the Town of Hunts Point.

the town, and provides just the measure of security that is needed. Hunts Point has gone as long as five years without a single home invasion burglary. It seems that privacy and security can be found without isolation. Hunts Point can remain a unique town in the larger region without cutting itself off from its neighbors.

HISTORY

Over the past 140 years Hunts Point has evolved from an almost unusable bit of wilderness into one of the most sought after communities in the Northwest; from the periphery of a rollicking frontier town to the very center of a dynamic modern metropolis. In the course of this journey, however, it never lost the fundamental character – woodsy, family-friendly, close-knit – that makes it so attractive today.

Although Seattle is very close - many residents can see it from their front windows – Hunts Point was among the last places on the Eastside to have permanent settlers. It turns out that the very characteristics that make it such prized real estate today – trees, waterfront, privacy – were not so valued 100 years ago. Hunts Point had neither the agricultural potential of Bellevue and Clyde Hill or the growing commuter population of Medina. Rather, Hunts Point started off as a place for vacation retreats. It evolved over the years in a unique way, and since incorporation the town has taken aggressive steps to lock in its sylvan character and to preserve those features that have given it such a strong sense of community.

Hunts Point residents dressed well for their 1915 Fourth of July celebration. Courtesy of the Town of Hunts Point.

Children stand at the Northup Dock in the late 1800s. Hunts Point is in the far background. Courtesy of King County Archives.

HUNTS POINT AND THE SETTLEMENT OF THE EASTSIDE

The story of Hunts Point begins with the larger story of the settlement of the lands to the east of Lake Washington. The Eastside today has more people than Seattle, but when settlers first started venturing across the lake, it was a remote wilderness. In the early 1880s, when the first permanent settlers were building farms and homes on the Eastside, Seattle's population was under 10,000, and most of the lands on the Seattle side of the lake remained logged off but unsettled, offering home sites close to town. The two mile trip across the lake by rowboat was formidable, especially when storms stirred up the lake. So it is little surprise that the Eastside developed slowly in the late 1800s: there were a lot of easier places to settle.

Some of the earliest permanent settlements on the Eastside were in the Houghton area, including that of Benson Northup, who built a home in the Yarrow Bay area in 1880. These early settlements contributed to Hunts Point's history in two important ways. First, Northup built a ferry wharf in the bay that attracted the early steamers on the lake. Because these boats had to pass the points on their way to their terminal in Madison Park it made sense to build wharfs on Yarrow, Hunts and Evergreen points. And if a passenger could not get to the wharf they could stand on their own dock and flag down a steamer: the private steamship operators were always eager for another fare.

The second important contribution of the Houghton settlements was establishment of a school. The Hunts Point-Houghton School District No. 22 dates back to 1878. Not many children would have travelled to Houghton from Hunts Point before Bay School was built in 1909, but the existence of a school of any kind indicates that the area was serious about being a place for families, and not just loggers and adventurers.

Hunts Point would also have been strongly influenced by the growth of what was the Eastside's largest town: Kirkland. While pioneer settlers were clustering around Houghton, bigger things were afoot just to the north. A Scotsman named Peter Kirk, aided by Leigh Hunt (who would give his name to Hunts Point) and other local and national investors, hatched a scheme to build a huge integrated iron and steel works in Washington, and eventually settled on a site near Forbes Lake in Kirkland's Rose Hill neighborhood. As the mill and its accompanying industries took shape in the early 1890s, thousands of people flocked to Moss Bay, and the town grew rapidly. A series of transportation problems, abetted by the financial panic of 1893, brought the entire enterprise to a halt, but not before Kirkland had established itself as the major urban area of the Eastside. Until Bellevue blossomed in the 1950s, Kirkland was the Eastside's most important center of commerce, and a road linked Hunts Point to Kirkland by 1912.

Ferry service on the lake consisted of privately owned steamers that could carry the occasional wagon or car, but mostly took just passengers. An early and important run was between Madison Park, in Seattle, and Houghton, and since the points were along with way, those needing a ride to Seattle could flag down a steamer. The first steamer to serve the area was the *Evril*, which began service to Houghton in 1883. As docks and cabins began to appear on Hunts Point it would have been served by vessels such as the sidewheeler *Kirkland*, which began serving Houghton in 1889, and the *City of Latona*, which served the Houghton run beginning in 1890.

The pace of development of the Central Eastside picked up significantly with the introduction of car ferry service on the *Leschi* in 1913.

The Leschi *provided the main link from the points communities to Seattle from 1913 to 1940. Courtesy of Puget Sound Maritime Historical Society.*

To serve the growing communities on Lake Washington the Port of Seattle decided to get into the ferry business, constructing the lake's first dedicated car ferry. The Port had a problem, though: it wanted to build a large steel hulled vessel. Up to that time the lake steamers had either been built at small yards on the lake or dragged up the Duwamish and Black Rivers at the south end of the lake (the Lake Washington Ship Canal was still on the drawing boards.). No yard on the lake could build a large steel hull, and the *Leschi* would be far too big to bring up the rivers. The solution was to assemble the hull temporarily at a yard along the Duwamish River in Seattle, dismantle it and haul the pieces to the lake and reassemble them there.

Once the *Leschi* was launched, she served a triangular route from the foot of Yesler Street in Seattle to Meydenbauer Bay in Bellevue then to Medina and back to Seattle. Within a few years the Port of Seattle decided to get out of the ferry business and sold the *Leschi* to Captain John Anderson, who was gradually gaining a near monopoly on the lake. Shortly after acquiring the route, Captain Anderson discontinued the Meydenbauer stop, making the cross-lake trip even faster.

The *Leschi's* Medina route continued to be the primary link between Seattle and the central Eastside until the Mercer Island bridge opened in 1940. For those taking a car to Seattle, Hunts Point was only about two miles from the Medina terminal, and four miles from the Kirkland dock, for those who preferred to land at Madison Park. After the *Les-*

Francis Boddy Road, now 84th Avenue NE, was originally a narrow dirt road, stretching from a wharf in Medina to a wharf on Cozy Cove. Courtesy of King County Archives.

chi discontinued its Medina route, it was shifted to the Kirkland route, where it served until 1950.

Although ferries and private boats on the lake provided the most reliable transportation system in the early decades of the Eastside, the road network gradually took shape, providing communities like Hunts Point with access to growing commercial centers like Kirkland and Bellevue.

Hunts Point Road was first carved out in 1905 and significantly improved in 1920. It connected to Francis Boddy Road (now 84th Avenue NE) which was established in 1898, providing access to the Medina ferry terminal and the Medina Grocery. The route to Kirkland ran along what is now Points Drive, which was created in 1912. Francis Boddy Road connected to Bellevue along Meydenbauer Bay by the late 1800s. So by the time that automobiles were becoming common, the Eastside had a serviceable road network and Hunts Point residents could meet more of their needs without venturing across the lake.

Today, although made up of many individual cities, each with its own identity, the Eastside does have its own sense of itself. The *Reflector* newspaper contributed importantly to that broading idea of an Eastside community. Published by the redoubtable H.Q. LeHuquet, the *Reflector* came out weekly from 1918 to 1934. Although based in Bellevue, it included news from all the communities south of Kirkland and north of Newcastle. Each community had its own weekly gossip items, and Hunts Point was part of the "Three Points" column. LeHuquet used his paper to boost the Eastside and push for improved schools, roads and community clubs. He was a tireless promoter of the nascent Bellevue high school and was dismayed that children from the points and elsewhere chose to go to High School elsewhere. The Reflector was followed by the larger Bellevue American which also provided ample coverage to event on the points.

As the Eastside was slowly growing in the early 1900s, Seattle was booming. A rough timber and fishing town for its first 50 years, the Klondike Gold Rush of 1897 led to a huge increase in population and economic activity. Seattle had just 37,000 people in 1890, and by 1910 the population was 237,000. This meant two things for the Eastside. First, there was a growing demand for agricultural products in the city. Much of the Eastside was carved out into farms that provided fresh fruits and vegetables, berries, dairy products and meat. Greenhouses, such as those operated in the Hunts Point area by the Boddy and Yabuki families, stretched the growing season.

The second impact, more important to Hunts Point, was the growing possibility of commuting to jobs in Seattle from outlying areas such as the Eastside. The trip by steamer from Hunts Point to the foot of Mad-

These greenhouses, standing where Medina Circle is today, were built by the Boddy family in the late 1800s and later bought by the Yabuki family. Courtesy of Washington State Archives.

ison St, took only 10 or 15 minutes, and with a trolley ride to downtown Seattle the total commute would take only about 45 minutes. By the 1920s, Medina, the points, Lochleven, Enetai and other areas near the lake that were not suited to agriculture had largely become commuter suburbs of Seattle. And the opening of the Mercer Island bridge in 1940 would only accelerate this evolution. The Eastside's massive residential growth of the 1950s and 1960s forced the final move away from agriculture and toward suburban living. Remaining farmlands were subdivided, and on waterfront properties large homes displaced summer cabins.

The consolidation of six school districts, including Hunts Point-Houghton and Medina, paved the way for a more integrated education system. Being part of the Overlake District, later named Bellevue School District 405, meant that Hunts Point children would attend high school in Bellevue instead of having a choice of going to Kirkland or even Seattle.

With the rapid post-war growth of housing in Lake Hills, Newport, Eastgate and other developments, the center of gravity of the Eastside shifted from Kirkland and Renton to Bellevue. And with Bellevue's incorporation in 1953, Hunts Point faced an important decision about its future as part of the Eastside. No longer an isolated lakefront neighborhood, Hunts Point had become part of a burgeoning suburban region that had very definite ideas about its future, and Hunts Point residents needed to decide how to fit into that future. In 1955 that decision process resulted in incorporation, and Hunts Point became one of what are now 15 cities and towns that make up the Eastside.

ORIGINS OF HUNTS POINT

Although it has some of the state's most valuable real estate today, Hunts Point would not have been considered prime property by the earliest settlers of the Eastside. The land was unsuitable for agriculture, so it could only be used for timber or home sites. Prior to the building of the Lake Washington Ship Canal and the Hiram M. Chittenden Locks, the lake level varied widely during the year, so Hunts Point's gently sloping shores meant a constantly changing beach and uncertain moorage.

No evidence has been found to date of permanent settlements by Native Americans on Hunts Point, but it certainly would have been a frequent stop for Salish people navigating the lake. The protected waters and gentle slopes and the lowlands at the head of Fairweather Bay and Cozy Cove would have provided easy access for seasonal hunting and fishing.

In the nineteenth century when white people from the east fanned out across the country the federal government devised ways to transfer land to individuals to encourage settlement. These transfers were known as "patents" and the two most common were homesteads and cash sales. A homestead patent required that the settler build a home on the property and live there for five years. The cash patent was much simpler: pay for the land.

The area that now comprises Hunts Point was settled under three separate patents. The largest was to Henry Nathan, Jr. who purchased almost all of Hunts Point and about half of Evergreen Point in May of 1869. His property extended from the base of Fairweather Bay on the south and the middle of Evergreen Point on the west, and took in all of Hunts Point except for a sliver on the east side. The reason he could not get the entire point was that the land patent process operated strictly within the "rectangular survey system" consisting of section, township and range designations. Since a line dividing two townships runs up the east side of the

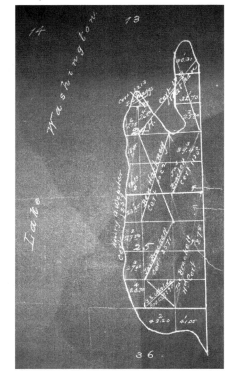

This map shows the original patents granted in the points area, with Henry Nathan having the patent for most of Hunts Point. Courtesy of Seattle Public Library.

Point, that eastern sliver was left to another settler.

That other settler was Neils Anderson, who took a homestead patent on all the land around Cozy Cove in 1889, extending to part of Yarrow Point and up Clyde Hill. Cozy Cove was long known as Anderson Bay. The area to the south of Fairweather Bay, now Hunts Point Circle and the Fairweather Yacht Basin, was part of a cash patent purchased by James Brackett in May of 1869.

It is not known what these men had in mind as they acquired land. Anderson would have been expected, as a homesteader, to improve his land, although most of it fell into the hands of Jacob Furth before long. Nathan and Brackett, as cash purchasers did not have the burden of improvements, and given that Henry Nathan took out two other patents on the same day for property in Seattle in what are now Laurelhurst and Windermere, the men may simply have been speculators. In any case, it appears from the 1898 survey for the Francis Boddy Road that the three original patentees had sold their holdings by then.

Things were slow during these decades as settlers struggled to find some way to make a living from the land. Around 1890, Francis Boddy purchased the land that is now Medina Circle from A.C. Anderson, who had acquired the original Brackett holdings that extended from

The Boddy family, who built this home just south of Hunts Point, were among the first permanent settlers in the area. Courtesy of Eastside Heritage Center.

Hunts Point south to NE 8th St, and included what is now the Over-lake Golf Course and Medina Park. Boddy began a dairy business with his three sons. He also built greenhouses and had a small sawmill.

Although the Boddy's original home burned, the family stuck around. The greenhouse operation was acquired by the Yabuki family in 1919, but the three brothers, Samuel, John and Albert retained the southern portion of the property and had additional land nearby on Clyde Hill. Albert Boddy served on the Hunts Point-Houghton School board from 1914 to 1923 and Sam Boddy is well remembered as the custodian of Bay School in the 1930s and 1940s.

Early census records show the area being called "Boddy," and what is now 84th Avenue was long known as Francis Boddy Road. Before the lowering of Lake Washington, Francis Boddy Road terminated in the north on Cozy Cove at a wharf known, not surprisingly, as Boddy Dock. And although the Boddys are long gone, the name still turns up on on-line map searches.

The 1890s bring us to the curious story of Leigh Hunt, the man whose name graces the Point, but who may never have set foot on it.

As the story on the following pages relates, Hunt became a wealthy man. To mark his success, he built a large home on the end of Yarrow Point. But as he sat on his verandah he found one disagreeable feature: trees blocking his view of the Olympic Mountains to the west. Those trees, of course, were on the end of the next point, and the only logical

Leigh Hunt built this home on the tip of Yarrow Point, and purchased Hunts Point so he could clear the trees and improve his view. Courtesy of Washington State Archives.

thing to do was to purchase the point and cut down the trees. Which he did, in 1888. Hunt suffered enormous financial setbacks in the years that followed and lost control of the Point, but not before giving it a name that would stick. Hunt's home still stands on the end of Yarrow Point.

Behind the now well-known story of Leigh Hunt was a character as influential in his time as Hunt, but considerably less dramatic: Jacob Furth. Furth was born in Bohemia and emigrated to the United States in 1856 at the age of 16. A confectioner by trade, he soon took up retailing, working his way from San Francisco to Nevada and finally to Seattle in 1882. Once in Seattle he raised $50,000 in capital to start the Puget Sound National Bank, which was an immediate success. He later invested heavily in streetcars and owned a large share of the interurban railways that traveled between Everett and Tacoma.

Like Hunt, Jacob Furth had diverse interests, and these included investment in real estate. In the 1880s he acquired most of Hunts Point, and was the owner who sold the tip to his business colleague Leigh Hunt. Furth retained the rest, selling it off one piece at a time. A 1905 map, surveyed for purposes of establishing Hunts Point Road,

Jacob Furth, a successful Seattle businessman, owned all of Hunts Point in the late 1800s as well as parts of what are now Yarrow Point and Clyde Hill. Courtesy of Museum of History & Industry.

Leigh S.J. Hunt

Hunts Point is named for Leigh S.J. Hunt, and though he never actually lived on the point, his story is worth telling, since it is intriguing and presages the kinds of stories heard on the point today. He was a key figure in Seattle business and politics in his day, and left many marks on history in Seattle, the U.S., and abroad. Though not without his detractors, and not without controversy, he was ultimately successful both personally and professionally, and is remembered for both his accomplishments and his large personality.

Hunt's Early Life

Smith James Hunt (he added the "Leigh" to his name in his early twenties) was born on August 11, 1855, one of twelve children born to Franklin and Martha Hunt in the tiny town of Etna, Indiana.

Hunt left the farm to become a teacher at a primary school when he was just seventeen years old, in 1872. Despite his lack of college education, he was soon he was leading lectures in the Whitley County Teachers' Institute, and became a high school principal in the larger community of Columbia City. He kept moving up in the world of education, serving as superintendent for East Des Moines Schools and as President of Iowa Agricultural College. His term as college president was not a particularly happy one, and by October 1885, he was already on his way out less than a year after taking the position.

While Hunt received honors and accolades in his teaching profession, his greatest talent was in networking and promoting his ideas. His mentors in Columbia City were staunch Republicans and soon Hunt was a passionate Republican and a firm believer in free enterprise. These passions for capitalism and politics would shape all that was to follow in his life.

Hunt in Seattle

Hunt's next move was to head west. He departed for Seattle in June 1886, and his wife Jessie and newborn son joined them shortly after. Soon after arriving in Seattle Hunt gained control of the Post-Intelligencer: his powers of persuasion once again landed him in a field in which he had no experience. Owning and operating a newspaper suited Hunt, and he used it to promote his many ideas and ambitions. By 1890, *Harper's* Magazine called the *P.I.* "one of the four great newspapers of the West Coast."

Hunt also used the paper to promote the Republican agenda that he was so passionate about, and it was observed that Hunt "came to Seattle on a Friday and ran its government by Saturday." Though he certainly had his supporters, his outspoken viewpoints – including speaking out against women's suffrage and in favor of a plan to return "negroes" to the Sudan – gained him many detractors.

Hunt soon decided to turn over the running of the newspaper, while maintaining ownership, in order to pursue investments and business in real estate and steel. In 1887 he began collaborating with Peter Kirk to create a steel industry that would make Seattle into the "Pittsburgh of the West." In tandem with his steel operation, Hunt set up a real estate business becoming the largest personal landowner on the Eastside.

By 1891, less than five years after leaving Iowa, Hunt was a wealthy man. But everything ended up depending on the success of the Kirkland steel mill, and things weren't going well. He was unsuccessful in getting the rail lines he needed and in completing the mill. In the midst of trying to get the steel enterprise going he began to invest in gold and silver claims in Monte Cristo, which also proved problematic.

By 1893 the mill and rail lines were completed and the mine at Monte Cristo was ready to go, both at great expense. But the timing could not have been much worse. There was a panic in 1893, and stocks were down drastically. Hunt was in financial trouble and had a hard time finding investors to keep afloat. As if these things were not enough, the mill at Kirkland was a failure: there were still problems getting ore to the mill and finished products to market.

Despite all of his earlier success, by 1894, Hunt was broke. He sold off his assets at a loss, letting go of the mill, his land company, and the *P.I.* He was even unable to retain the property that came to bear his name, forfeiting the deed to Hunt's Point back to its original owner, Jacob Furth. It appeared that Hunt was finished in Seattle, and he conceded that if he stayed, he would "starve or die of boredom. Accordingly, Hunt declared that he must leave Seattle, and he left to pursue new adventure, business, and opportunity in the Far East.

Hunt's Seattle story does not end here, however. In 1901, he returned to Seattle, having made a new fortune operating mines in Korea. Although the statute of limitations lifted his debt obligations, Hunt had other ideas. He threw a banquet for his old friends and repaid all of them with interest! There was only one exception to his repayment: to his old friend, Jacob Furth, he refused to pay interest. Furth was the only friend to refuse Hunt's invitation to dine, and the bond between them was never healed.

By the time of Hunt's death, in 1933, he had learned to hold on to his wealth, and he had made indelible marks on national and international history. He was a personal advisor to President Theodore Roosevelt, he helped to colonize the Sudan, he explored regions of Asia (including Korea) previously unknown to white men, and he eventually settled in Las Vegas as a real estate man, where he successfully worked until his dying day.

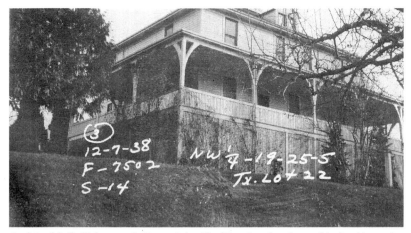

Jacob Furth built this home on the Yarrow Point side of Cozy Cove, later bequeathing it to his grand-daughters, the Wetherill sisters. Courtesy of Washington State Archives.

shows Furth still controlling a large share of Hunts Point. An 1898 map shows that he also owned, along with Baily Gazert, land to the east of Boddy Road on Clyde Hill and on the east side of Cozy Cove, where he built a home in 1892. Furth died in 1914 and by 1917 nearly all his holdings on Hunts Point had been sold. Most of his land along Cozy Cove, with the exception of the Bay School site (now Hunts Point Town Hall), remained in the hands of the Puget Sound National Bank. He did, however, retain the property that would eventually pass down to his granddaughters, the Wetherill sisters, who would subsequently donate that land to Hunts Point and Yarrow Point for the Wetherill Nature Preserve.

Around 1900, when the Point was still largely undeveloped, James Brewster purchased a 10-acre summer campsite on the tip that Hunt had cleared. Living a rustic tent life for two seasons, he built a large home and began the trend of country estates on the Eastside. When his children were old enough to live on their own, he built each of them a house nearby, one on the east and one on the west side of the point. Brewster owned a demolition company in Seattle, and demolitions by Brewster's company were said to be the source of bricks used in many Hunts Point homes, notably the home of his daughter, Helen Brewster Buzard, where many Town Council meetings were held.

James Brewster built this home at the tip of Hunts Point and became among the first year-round residents. Courtesy of Washington State Archives.

From the late 1800s to the early 1900s Hunts Point would be gradually divided up into parcels that, in large part, have remained to this day. By 1911 the county assessor had surveyed the area and established an "Assessor's Plat of Hunts Point" that officially recorded all parcels. Although by the early 1900s land developers had platted parts of Medina into conventional subdivisions with small, regular lots, Hunts Point was carved up into strips extending from the ridge all the way to

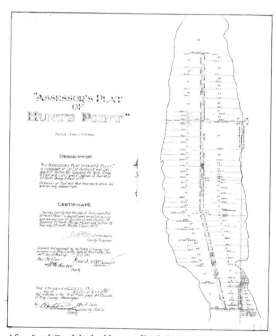

After Jacob Furth had sold most of his holdings bit by bit, the County Assessor created a formal plat to recognize these new parcels and fix their boundaries. Courtesy of King County Archives.

the water, a pattern that remains today.

In the early days Hunts Point served as a summer retreat from the rapidly urbanizing life of Seattle, and most landowners put up simple cabins and small houses that would be comfortable during the warm months of the year. Husbands could easily commute to Seattle by steamer and children could entertain themselves in the lake and woods. When the cold weather and lake storms arrived, families would return to Seattle with its well-appointed schools, warm homes and wintertime activities.

The crucial comforts of living that would make the Point a better year-round residence began to arrive in the early 20th Century. Puget Sound Power and Light installed electric service in 1910, but it was quite expensive. Phone service arrived a few years later, and a typhoid scare in 1922 led to the construction of a water system with a pump house at what is now 3655 Hunts Point Road.

Away from the Point and the amenities of the lake the land was still pretty raw. The Bechtel family, Canadians who settled near Meydenbauer Bay, had logged off much of the area in the 1880s, leaving stumps, weeds and immature trees. The photo of Blomskag Road (now NE 28th Street east of 84th Avenue) in 1905 shows a landscape that would not exactly inspire the poets: scrubby deciduous trees along with fir

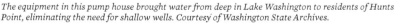

The equipment in this pump house brought water from deep in Lake Washington to residents of Hunts Point, eliminating the need for shallow wells. Courtesy of Washington State Archives.

and hemlock that were dead or too small to harvest. It would take many years and a lot of work to transform the area into the sylvan paradise of today.

GETTING TO AND AROUND HUNTS POINT

For the earliest settlers on the east side of Lake Washington, the primary mode of transportation was the lake itself. Most early homes were built near the lake, and every lakefront home had a dock. Homes were oriented toward the water, with the "front" door on the lake side, since most visitors would arrive by boat. In some areas home sites came with easements across the lakeshore that required

This photo of the right of way for Blomskag Road, now NE 28th Street between 84th Avenue and 92nd Avenue, shows the rough landscape after the area had been logged. Courtesy of King County Archives.

residents to keep an open path for their neighbors to use to get to the nearest ferry dock.

Ferries

The earliest settlers on the lake had only their own rowboats to get to and from their neighbors or to Seattle. The first passenger steamer, the *Evril*, appeared on the lake in 1883, making runs between Houghton and Madison Park, and within a few years several boats were taking passengers around the lake. These boats had two lines of business. The real money was made with chartered trips for groups from Seattle. Moonlight cruises, parties and other excursions were popular, setting out from the main wharfs at Leschi, Madrona and Madison Park.

The second, more difficult business, was taking passengers around the lake. Before Captain John Anderson consolidated services, the ferries were independently owned and the business was completely unregulated, leading to fierce competition and less than honest practices of poaching passengers. Operators with thin income could not maintain their vessels as well as they should have, and fires, rot and sinkings were common. Despite this chaos in the marketplace, the ferries provided the essential transportation needed along the lake.

The points communities had a series of ferry wharfs for regular service. These included docks at Northup, near Carillon Point and three wharfs on the Yarrow Point side of Cozy Cove: Yarrow, Sunnyside and Stevens. The earliest ferry dock on Hunts Point would have been the Boddy Wharf at the north end of Francis Boddy Road, about where 3268 Hunts Point Road is today. As more customers lived on the Point, more ferry landings were built: a 1934 Kroll map of Hunts Point shows Penrose Landing and Greenwood Landing on Cozy Cove, and Fairweather Landing and Clubhouse landing on Fairweather Bay. Residents on the points knew that if they missed the ferry on one side of the point they could dash to a wharf on the other side and hope to catch the ferry as it rounded the point.

The passenger steamer business was always changing, so it is difficult to know all the boats that served Hunts Point. One resident who

Sunnyside Landing, on the Yarrow Point side of Cozy Cove, served steamers on the Houghton-Madison Park run. Courtesy of Washington State Archives.

Penrose Landing, at what is now 4038 Hunts Point Road, served the north side of the point on Cozy Cove. Courtesy of Washington State Archives.

The Dawn served many parts of Lake Washington, including Houghton and the Points. Courtesy of Eastside Heritage Center.

moved to Hunts Point in 1910 recalls seeing the *Atlanta*, the *Fortuna*, the *Aquila* and the *Dawn*.

The last steamer to provide passenger service on Lake Washington, the much beloved *Ariel*, began service between Houghton and the points and Madison Park in 1921 and made its last run in May, 1945. Many current and former residents of the points have fond memories of Henry and Marcus Johnson, the brothers who owned the *Ariel*, and of the charming trips across the lake. The Johnson brothers had the distinction of being the only operators never to sell their boat to Cap-

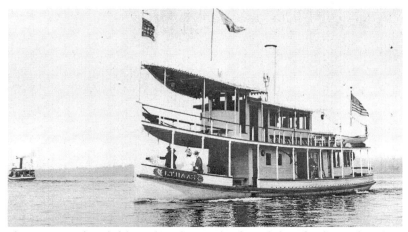

The L.T. Haas *mostly worked the Leschi-Medina route but also worked out of Madison Park, serving Houghton and Kirkland. Courtesy of Puget Sound Maritime Historical Society.*

The Ariel was the last steamer to serve on Lake Washington. She made a regular run from Houghton to Madison Park by way of the points from 1921 to 1945. Courtesy of Puget Sound Maritime Historical Society.

tain Anderson, who gradually gained control of all steamship service on Lake Washington.

Once in Seattle, steamer passengers could get a quick ride to downtown Seattle aboard the streetcar. Most Hunts Point passengers would land at the foot of Madison Street and catch the streetcar that ran the length of Madison Street to downtown. Madison Park was among the first of Seattle's "streetcar suburbs," so ferry passengers were greeted by a well-developed community and frequent streetcar service.

In this photo from the early 1930s the Ariel is leaving Madison Park, heading to the points. The tip of Hunts Point is seen to the right of the diving platform. Courtesy of City of Seattle Archives.

The ferry wharfs on the east side were another matter entirely. Most of the docks were built and owned by King County, but the county was not very good about maintaining them. The piers and decks were built of wood, mostly untreated, and the docks tended to rot easily. Survey reports from the County Engineer's office report deteriorating piers and generally unsafe conditions. Nonetheless, the county piers were the lifeline to the big city across the lake.

Roads

In the early days, the story of roads on Hunts Point was simple: one road. The Hunts Point Road of today, which is among the more delightful arterials in the region, is the fourth version of this road.

In the late 1800s most movement and commerce in the area happened along the water, so the earliest settlers had little need for a real road. They did create trails or rough tracks along the ridge of the Point, demarcating property that had already been carved up along that north-south axis. The first formal road was built by King County in 1905, and was named for the property owner who first petitioned the county: F.F. French. The road later became known as County Road No. 817. Francis Boddy Road, which is now 84th Avenue, was already built by that time, as was the route along Meydenbauer Bay to Bellevue. This new road would, therefore, connect to an established road network providing access to Medina and Bellevue. With the completion in 1912 of the Medina-Kirkland road, now known as Points Drive, Hunts Point would be connected by land to Kirkland.

The process to build a new public road in the wilderness began with a petition to the County Commission from at least 10 property owners who would benefit from the new road. If the petition met the county's requirements, the commission issued an Order for Examination to the County Engineer, instructing him to survey the proposed road. The engineer would verify the affected property owners, measure the amount of land each would be required to contribute to the right of way, and make a recommendation that the road is "a necessity and ought to be established and opened." The box shows the names of the those who signed the petition in 1905, including F.F. French, the lead petitioner, who owned a parcel on the west side of the Point.

The proposed F.F. French road passed the test. After surveying the land in August, 1905, the County Engineer recommended that a 30-foot right of way be established. The survey found that the property owners with just a single strip of land would be contributing 0.2 acres to the right of way, but that Jacob Furth, who still had substantial holdings on Hunts Point, would be contributing 2.63 acres.

In 1905 the following property owners on Hunts Point petitioned the County Commission to build what would later become Hunts Point Road

Richard Weller	W. H. Sanders
Olive Coe	John Shaw
E.S. Goodwin	E.H. Ahrens
E.L. Drew	F.W. Hurlburt
H.C. McDonald	J. Furth
I.H. Jennings	F.B, Shell
W.B. Judah	Lilian Brysland
Fred Everett	Mary Hardy
R.H. Chadwick	Adeline Buxman
H.C. McDonald	Katherine Mayo
D.J. Burkhart	Helen Ziegler
M.S. Thomson	E. Hughes
Nancy Howard	A.C. Anderson
G.H. Tripp	E.A. Chushill
E. von Norman	J. Dalton
W.G. Booth	O. von Norman
Geo. Bradley	F.F. French

F F French Road   Sec. 13. 25. 4

This photo shows FF French Road, now Hunts Point Road, during construction. Courtesy of King County Archives.

The next step was to get the property owners to sign over their piece of the right of way. This was done through quit claim deeds that promised the property owner "one dollar and also the benefits to accrue to them by reason of laying out and establishing a public road through their property . . ." The property owners all duly signed their quit claim deeds and the county proceeded with construction of F.F French Road.

The 1905 Engineers report shows that all of the property owners listed their main address as Seattle or somewhere else. None of the owners appear to have been permanent residents, so they were either seasonal residents or had no improvements on their property at all. In this case, a gravel road on a 30-foot right of way would have been just fine. But by 1920 the Point had more permanent residents and needed a larger right of way.

And so the process started over again. The County Engineer surveyed the road and determined which property owners would need to contribute an additional 10 feet of their property on either side of the existing street to create a 50 foot right of way. The engineer recommended widening the road and the property owners again deeded over their strips of land. But this road only went as far as the current 4204 Hunts Point Road. In 1937 the county extended the road another 757 feet to its current terminus.

The original 16 foot concrete pavement of Hunts Point Road lasted until 2005 when it was replaced with an 18 foot road that looks remarkably similar. The 1920 road was built by the Nordstrom Company, although that firm appears to have no relationship to the Nordstroms that now live in Hunts Point.

While Hunts Point Road remains largely in the form it had by 1920, another major

Fairweather Wharf, at the head of Fairweather Bay, was accessed from the Boddy Hindle trestle. Courtesy of King County Archives.

road project has mostly disappeared. In 1918 the county decided that a ferry wharf was needed at the foot of Fairweather Bay. Lake Washington had just been lowered, making most existing wharfs and docks unusable, so new ferry access was needed. Although the head of the bay was now a wetland, the county saw that location as a proper one for a ferry. The problem was getting through the marsh to the water.

The solution was the Boddy Hindle road and trestle, named for the two main roads on either end: Francis Boddy Road and Hindle Road (now Evergreen Point Road). The plan was to start at Boddy Road and build a raised trestle across the wetland between Hunts Point and Evergreen Point, with a branch to the north for the ferry wharf at the head of Fairweather Bay. Since this project was driven by the need for a county-owned ferry wharf, the petition process was simpler. There were only four affected property owners along the right of way, and each deeded over the required land.

The head of Fairweather Bay however, turned out to be a poor location for a ferry wharf. Few people lived in the area and those that did could easily walk to wharfs further out on the points or make their way to the faster car ferry in Medina. The county wharf inspectors report of 1930 describes the dock as rotted everywhere above the waterline. Within a few years the wharf was entirely gone, not appearing at all on the 1937 aerial photos of the area.

The Boddy-Hindle road and trestle, however, were well used, especially by students attending Bay School, which was located near the east end of the road. The wood pilings deteriorated, and in 1944 the structure was replaced with fill taken from the grading and construction of NE 28th Street. But it was construction of the Fairweather Yacht Basin in 1957 that doomed the road, as the head of the bay was filled in and dredged for new home sites and the new Town of Hunts Point vacated the right of way. NE 32nd Street in Medina and a section of Hunts Point Circle are all that remain of the road today. While stabilizing Fairweather Place in 2006, the Town Engineer found remnants of the rotted trestle, which had to be removed at an unexpected expense.

Hunts Point Circle was laid out as part of a formal subdivision, Hunts Point Park Addition, in 1951, and Fairweather Place was part of the Fairweather Basin subdivision completed in 1957. The last piece of the road network, Hunts Point Lane, was built in Cozy Cove as part of the final land development in Hunts Point, in 1976.

This photo shows the Boddy Hindle Trestle under construction, viewed from Hunts Point, across Fairweather Bay to Evergreen Point. The trestle to Fairweather Wharf branches to the right. Courtesy of King County Archives.

This view of the Boddy Hindle Trestle is taken from the Evergreen Point side, looking toward Hunts Point. Courtesy of King County Archives.

RESHAPING THE LAKE

The geography of Hunts Point has been shaped by two significant changes in the lakeshore. The first of these occurred in 1917 when the lake was lowered by about nine feet to bring it level with the new Lake Washington Ship Canal. The second change happened in the mid-1950s when the Fairweather Yacht Basin was dredged out of the marsh at the head of Fairweather Bay.

Lowering the lake

Prior to the opening of the ship canal, Lake Washington was not only higher, but also varied in height during the year. The lake drained to the south, through the Black River, which ran about where the Boeing plant sits in Renton. The Black River, in turn, connected to the Duwamish in Tukwila. During the winter, when rains were heavy, and during the spring when snowmelt came down the Cedar and Sammamish rivers, the Black River could not drain the lake fast enough, and the level would rise. During the summer, when the snowmelt slowed, the Black River would catch up, and the lake level would fall. With the gentle slopes of Hunts Point, waterfront property owners could see the water's edge shift noticeably during the year.

The Lake Washington Ship Canal was conceived during a period of great growth and optimism about the future of the Seattle area, and proponents envisioned major industrial development throughout Lake Washington. As an example of this, the Bogue Plan, drawn up for the City of Seattle in 1911, shows an industrial district in Yarrow Bay. Although some industrial development did occur on the lake, such as the whaling station in Meydenbauer Bay, the enlargement of the shipyard in Houghton and a major sawmill in Kenny-

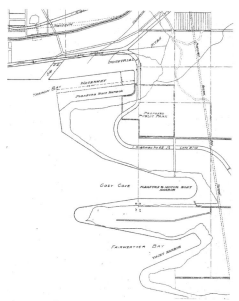

The Bogue Plan, drawn up by the Seattle Plans Commission in 1911, envisioned yacht harbors in both Fairweather Bay and Cozy Cove, but a more industrial use of Yarrow Bay. Courtesy of Seattle Public Library.

dale, areas such as Fairweather Bay and Cozy Cove were spared industrialization (The Bogue Plan envisioned them as yacht harbors).

The lowering of the lake did, however, have a major impact on waterfront homes, opening a new shelf of land along the shore. At first this was a major problem, since all the docks on which residents depended were left high and dry. The newly exposed lake bottom was at best dirty, and at worst, smelly as underwater growth rotted in the sun. And property owners were not automatically entitled to this new land – they had to buy it from the county!

The new land did make Hunts Point larger than before, with the point extending out about another 400 feet. Most lakefront property owners added between 25 and 50 feet to their strips of land. Cozy Cove and Fairweather Bay shrank by about 600 feet, and new marshlands grew in the stream deltas exposed at their heads.

The new canal did provide much-needed stability to the lake level. The dam at the Hiram M. Chittenden Locks has been used ever since to regulate the water level in Lake Washington. The lake is kept lower in the winter to accommodate surges of stormwater and to protect beaches when waves kick up in wind storms. In the spring the Army Corps of Engineers, which operates the canal, raises the lake level to provide enough water to operate the locks. In all, the lake now varies only about two feet during the year.

The ship canal did allow larger vessels to be brought into Lake Washington. Prior to the canal, boat were either built on the lake or dragged up the Black River. Navigating the Black River was not easy: wait until high tide on the Duwamish and hope for a surge of water to fill the river and then get a team of oxen to pull the boat across the sandbars. With the canal the lake could have a larger fleet of passenger steamers and barges to serve waterfront homes. For Hunts Point, the canal has mostly meant allowing waterfront home owners to use their docks for pleasure boats that can get to the salt water for extended cruising.

Fairweather Yacht Basin

Creation of the Fairweather Yacht Basin in the mid-1950s marked the second major change to the Hunts Point shoreline. This project turned a little-used marshland into prime real estate.

The Yabuki family, which lived in this home just south of Hunts Point, farmed the lowlands at the head of Fairweather Bay until they were dredged for the Fairweather Yacht Basin. Courtesy of the Washington State Archives.

The glaciers that carved out the topography of the Puget Sound area tended to leave gentle slopes on the north-south axis and steeper slopes on the east-west axis. Thus, the original grade of Fairweather Bay featured a gradual slope from the south into the bay, and a shallow slope underwater. This made for a marshy shore land as the lake varied during the year, and when the lake was permanently lowered, a large flat area was exposed similar to what is found in the Mercer Slough in Bellevue.

As seen in this 1936 aerial photo the head of Fairweather Bay consisted of marsh and farmland. The new yacht basin would extend nearly to the bottom of this photo. Courtesy of King County Department of Transportation.

The aerial photo from 1937 shows that some of this area was farmed (mostly by the Yabuki family) but much was left untouched. The photo also shows the Boddy-Hindle trestle cutting through. This topography remained largely unchanged until the mid-1950s when an investor group saw the potential to turn a "mosquito patch with weeds and rats" into a residential community.

Since there was far less resistance to filling in wetlands in those days, the biggest issue for the developers was the required vacation of the old Boddy Hindle Road that went through the proposed subdivision. The dredged basin would slice through the road making it useless, so the developers sought to close the road and acquire the land under it. They had submitted a request for vacation to the County Commission, but incorporation changed the ownership of the road from the county to the new town. The newly organized Town of Hunts Point found a complex project on its agenda within a month of incorporation.

The Town Council, while generally favoring the project, had some concerns. They had envisioned keeping the entrance to Hunts Point limited to just Hunts Point Road, and at that time, entry from the west would have been possible. To ensure a single entrance, no road was built along the south side of Fairweather Basin, making the homes on the west side accessible only through Medina.

In 1965, when this photo was taken, the area around the Fairweather Yacht Basin was still largely unbuilt. Courtesy of Washington State Archives.

A second issue was sewers. In the mid-1950s all communities along the lake were battling pollution caused by inadequate sewage treatment which was making the lake unsafe. The low, soft ground in Fairweather Bay would not have been conducive to septic systems, so although the land could be developed, actual homebuilding had to wait several years for sewers to serve the area.

After what, by today's standards, was a fairly short period of review by the Planning Commission and Town Council, the development was approved. But although the route of SR 520 was clearly laid out by then, the plat for Fairweather Basin Addition was extended across the future freeway right of way to NE 28th Street. Homebuilding was slow, with just a handful of houses built in the first ten years. The final vacant lot was built on in 2004, and the two southernmost homes were acquired by the State Department of Transportation in 2009 as part of the SR 520 expansion project.

The Hunts Point market was the central gathering place of the community, standing the intersection of Francis Boddy Road and Blomskag Road -- today right at the eastbound offramp from SR 520. Courtesy of Washington State Archives.

BUSINESSES ON HUNTS POINT

Hunts Point today is known as a town with no visible commercial enterprises, which is not surprising given its physical geography. But there have been a few businesses and farms over the years.

The first, and probably largest, enterprises in the Hunts Point area were established by the Boddy family on lands near the base of Hunts Point. The Yabuki family took over the Boddy farm and extended it into the lowlands of Fairweather Bay. The Yabukis were among the

The Overlake Garage, at the northwest corner of Points Drive and 88th Avenue, served early car owners of Hunts Point. Courtesy of Washington State Archives

This gas and service station stood on the site that Tullys occupies in Clyde Hill. Courtesy of Washington State Archives.

few Japanese-American families to return to the area after their internment during World War II, and even after the SR 520 freeway ended farming in Fairweather Bay, they kept operating their greenhouses into the 1970s.

Retail services on Hunts Point were always limited. An early general store was located on Harry Hurlbut's dock on Cozy Cove at what is now 3858 Hunts Point Road (the original building still exists and is one of a handful of grandfathered structures allowed in front of the stringline). To better serve his customers, Hulbert began running a floating grocery story, the Grubstake, along the lakeshore. In his two-lung diesel boat he picked up his stock in Bothell and covered the points along his route. While much of his fresh food was greatly appreciated in places with few other resources, many complained that the bread he sold had a taste of diesel exhaust!

A larger grocery and gas station operated just north of the Boddy/ Yabuki greenhouses, about where the eastbound off-ramp from SR 520 is located today. The store was started by Stanley and Christina Norman, who expanded it from a small one-room shop to a larger operation. After the Normans, the Mooreheads and various other families owned the business until its closing in 1961. The store was a much beloved institution in Hunts Point, but, sadly, sat in the middle of the new freeway project.

Just outside of Hunts Point, on Points Drive, a service station located on the site of Tully's Coffee provided more elaborate car repairs.

Another sources of supplies would have been the Medina Grocery. Although a couple of miles away by poor roads, it was still the nearest grocery to Hunts Point in the early days. When the Hagenstein family took over the newly established grocery in 1908 they had a very limited customer base, and soon learned that delivery of a wide range of items, such as fuel and animal feed, was necessary to keep the business afloat. Despite its distance, Hunts Point would have been on their delivery route.

CREATING A COMMUNITY

During the first half of the 20th Century just a few miles across the water to the west, Seattle was becoming a major city, with all of the institutions and amenities one expects in a large urban area. The Eastside was, however, still a sort of frontier where residents had to create their own institutions and social infrastructure out of nothing but a desire for community. Central to this process were schools and community clubs. Bellevue had schools from early on and formed a thriving community club (its clubhouse on 100th Avenue was later the original Bellevue Boys Club). Medina formed its own school district in 1910 and had an active Improvement Club. Similarly, Hunts Point residents built a school and very successful clubhouse. A new sense of community gave rise to a unique institution – Clean Up Day – that continues today.

School on Hunts Point

Until the mid-1900s, most rural areas of the state were divided into very small individual school districts, mostly with a single building. Each district had its own school board and controlled its own property tax base. This worked adequately for elementary grades, as primary schools are easy and inexpensive to operate. The central Eastside had quite a few of these districts, the oldest being Houghton, formed in 1878. Other districts served Bellevue (1886), Phantom Lake (1893), Factoria (1901), Highland (1889) and Medina (1910).

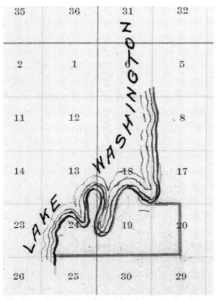

The Hunts Point-Houghton School District No. 22 covered the points north of what is now 24th Street, extending east to what is today 116th Avenue. Courtesy of Washington State Archives.

High school was more problematic for these rural areas. Then, as now, families expected a higher level of educational sophistication in high school, as well as sports and other extracurricular activities that small districts could not easily provide. The solution was for high school students from small districts to travel to a high school outside their district, to which their home district paid a fee. Many students from Medina took the ferry to Seattle and attended Garfield High School. Students from the points had this option, but more likely traveled to Kirkland, which had a well established high school. (A Yabuki family photo shows a young man wearing a sweater with a large K for Kirkland High School.)

In 1923 several Eastside districts (not including Hunts Point-Houghton or Medina) joined forces to create the Union S High School, which would have been an easier option for Hunts Point children. But until the new brick building was built in 1930, it would have compared poorly to Kirkland High School. The Union S building later became Bellevue Junior High School, and was demolished to make way for the Bellevue Downtown Park.

In the late 19th and early 20th Centuries the state conducted an annual "Census of children between the ages of five and twenty-one" by school district. In the Census of Children for 1900, for School District No. 22 there appear to be no children residing permanently in Section 24, which consisted of Hunts Point and Evergreen Point, south to 24th Street. Families mostly lived on Hunts and Evergreen points during

The imposing Houghton School is shown in the distance from the Northup Wharf in Yarrow Bay. Courtesy of King County Archives.

the summer, but retreated to Seattle for the school year. Six families with a total of 17 children, including Francis Boddy's daughter, lived in Section 20 which encompassed Yarrow Point and Clyde Hill north of 24th Street.

In the next ten years, however, the schoolchildren arrived. By the 1909 Census of Children, there were eight households permanently residing in Section 24 with a total of 19 children. This baby boom included the Hurlbut children, Wade, Robert and Elizabeth, as well as the

Bay School opened in 1910 on the site that Hunts Point Town Hall now occupies. Courtesy of Washington State Archives.

By the 1930s, Bay School had expanded to six classrooms. Courtesy of Washington State Archives.

Brewster children, Jason and Helen, and Robert Burkhart. All of these families appear on early maps of Hunts Point. Section 24 also included Evergreen Point, where a few hardy families were building permanent homes.

The 1909 Census of Children listed a total of 68 children in District No. 22, which stretched from Houghton to Evergreen Point and was served by just one school which was located near today's Carillon Point. It was clearly time to build a new school closer to the growing points communities. Unlike Medina, which had been part of Bellevue School District No. 49 and opted to break off and form its own district in 1910, Hunts Point stayed with the Houghton district.

To get the new school going, Jacob Furth deeded over a parcel of land at the base of the Point, where the current Town Hall now stands. The building was completed in 1909 and Bay School had its first class of about 10 students. The original building, shown in the photo, had just one room and one teacher. Bay School grew steadily as an increasing number of families made the points and Clyde Hill their year-round home. The building was expanded in 1919 and 1938. By the late 1930s it had six classrooms, a lunchroom, a large outdoor shed and an extensive playground.

In the late 1930s the Houghton-Hunts Point and Medina school districts began working together to offer more comprehensive elemen-

Bay School student body of 1933. Courtesy of William Coffin.

tary education. Under the new arrangement children in grades one through three from both districts would attend Medina School, on the site of the current Medina Elementary, and children in grades four through six from both districts would attend classes at Bay School. This allowed for larger classes and more attention from teachers.

In 1942 six districts on the Eastside – Bellevue, Hunts Point-Houghton, Medina, Phantom Lake Factoria and Highland – combined to form the new Overlake School District (later named Bellevue School District 405). In the new unified district Hunts Point children would attend the Union S High School in Bellevue, cutting the last tie between Hunts Point and Kirkland, which had been the original Eastside metropolis but was about to be eclipsed by Bellevue. The new district also set a precedent for areas of the central Eastside to work together, a precedent that would color the incorporation efforts of the following decade.

Tragedy struck on May 31, 1950 when Bay School caught fire. Neighbors made a valiant effort to put the fire out, but their effort was futile, and the cherished building burned to the ground. The school's 89 students finished the year at Overlake Elementary School (also on the

Three Point School served Hunts Point children from 1961 to 1981. Courtesy of Washington State Archives.

site of the Bellevue Downtown Park) and were sent to other schools the following year as the school district decided what to do next. Plans were already on the drawing boards for a second Lake Washington bridge, and a favored location was across the Points, putting the site of Bay School potentially in the path. The district decided not to rebuild on Hunts Point and concentrated on its building plan for other sites.

The closest school for students on Hunts Point was Medina, but that building was already bursting at the seams. With rapid growth throughout the Eastside, however, the district had big plans for new and expanded schools. The first new school in the points area was Clyde Hill Elementary, which opened in 1952, providing the nearest elementary school to Hunts Point. An expanded Medina Elementary School opened in 1957, and Ashwood Elementary, located where the Bellevue library sits today, opened in 1956. Bellevue High School moved to a new building on its current site in 1949, allowing Bellevue Junior High School to occupy the old Union S building. Chinook Junior High School, which still serves Hunts Point, opened on Clyde Hill in 1961.

1961 was also the year that the points finally got a new elementary school: Three Points Elementary. This new school served students from Hunts, Yarrow and Evergreen points, covering about the same territory as Bay School. The history of Three Points is short, however, since the district closed it in 1981. By the time Three Points had opened, the baby boom of the points communities was peaking, and the wave of children that moved into new homes in the 1950s and 1960s was rapidly heading off to junior high school and high school. The Points were becoming neighborhoods of empty nesters, with many fewer children heading off to elementary school. Shortly after closing, the Three Points campus was leased to Bellevue Christian School to serve as its new elementary school. Although elementary boundaries shift, Hunts Point children have mostly been assigned to Clyde Hill elementary since the closing of Three Points.

The Hunts Point Tennis Club

In an isolated community such as the early Hunts Point, social life had to be created from the ground up. Improvement and community clubs flourished across the Eastside, and Hunts Point founded its own club – the Hunts Point Tennis Club – in 1908. And it did not take long to get a clubhouse built. When the Brewster family no longer allowed open access to their tennis courts on the end of the Point, Lee Clark collected one hundred dollars from each family on the Point to build a clubhouse. The new club site had dirt tennis courts and a large hall with a stove, a kitchen and a stage. Dances were held regularly and even a wedding occurred at the clubhouse The original clubhouse was located at what is now 3655 Hunts Point Road.

The Hunts Point Tennis Club was the center of community activity from 1908 to the late 1920s. Courtesy of the Town of Hunts Point.

The Hunts Point Howler, an eight page newspaper printed entirely in red ink, provided a light-hearted look at Hunts Point life for the 1922 Ja Ba Wa Ka Jinx celebration. Courtesy of Eastside Heritage Center.

Club life reached perhaps its high point in 1921 and 1922 with the festivities of Ja Ba Wa Ka Jinx (the name taken from the Jabberwocky in Lewis Carroll's Through the Looking Glass). For the day-long festival every resident of the Point had a job and at the end of the day each year, the festival had raised over $1,000 to help pay off the mortgage on the clubhouse.

The clubhouse served as the focal point for social life in Hunts Point, and since even then the residents were relatively well-to-do, events and activities were elaborate. The annual Fourth of July celebration featured a tennis tournament, boat races a picnic and fireworks display. But as one resident at the time recalled, it was the opening of the Overlake Golf and Country Club in 1925, supported by many Hunts Point residents, that signaled the decline of the clubhouse as the center of social life. The Tennis Club folded in the late 1920s and the clubhouse was sold. The Improvement Committee did, however, remain in existence and led the incorporation movement in the 1950s.

The Improvement Committee and Clean up Day

Every strong community has its touchstones and its rituals that define its values and provide common reference points. In Hunts Point,

that would be Clean Up Day. It
might seem ironic that a pros-
perous community defines itself
by rolling up its sleeves, but that
is exactly the idea: taking care of
common spaces gives residents
a unique ownership of the town,
and turning the day into a social
event brings newcomers together
with long-time residents.

*The Pop Truck has been a fixture of Clean Up
day for decades. Courtesy of the Town of Hunts
Point.*

It all started in 1920, when the Hunts Point Improvement Committee issued a call to residents to clean up the property along the road.
Hunts Point Road had just been widened and paved, and residents saw
a need to maintain the foliage around it. The Committee also commissioned mailbox stands and planted trees where they were needed.

*Hunts Point residents, left to right, Don Jasper,
Michael Kliott, Jim Schneider and Ernie
Norehad at Clean Up Day in 2005. Courtesy of
Town of Hunts Point.*

The event has been happening
ever since, on the third Sunday in
May, rain or shine. Dumpsters are
placed along the right-of-way and
residents all pitch in trimming
trees and shrubs, cleaning up
brush and trash. The "pop truck"
drives through the town with cold
drinks, and the day concludes
with a cocktail party, hosted by
the newest members of the com-
munity. For long time residents, one of the most memorable Clean Up
days occurred on May 18, 1980, when participants were startled by the
boom of the Mount St. Helens eruption.

MID-CENTURY CHANGES

The shift of Hunts Point from a relatively isolated community to a vibrant suburban town began one day in 1940, when the new Mercer
Island floating bridge opened. As long as traveling to Seattle required
a ferry trip, Eastside living had a limited appeal: the delights of the

This 1936 aerial photo of Hunts Point, Yarrow Point and Clyde Hill shows just how wooded and rural the area was, and how ripe for development it looked in the eyes of homebuilders. Courtesy of PEMCO Webster & Stevens Collection, Museum of History & Industry.

points communities came at the price of a complicated commute. But with easy new driving and bus routes to Seattle, Eastside living became more attractive and homebuilding took off.

Although on the periphery of the post-war rush of homebuilding happening across the Eastside, the points could not entirely escape. In 1950 the prominent Eastside development firm of Bell and Valdez submitted a plat for the Hunts Point Park Addition: 38 lots under the county's R-1 zoning district. These lots were as small as 10,000 square feet, which was a far cry from the large parcels on the Point, and were clustered around a standard "suburban" street.

But more than just introducing a new type of homesite to the area, Hunts Point Park fundamentally changed the geography of what the residents had come to know as Hunts Point. For many years an entry monument stood at the corner of Hunts Point Road and the Boddy Hindle Road (site of the current stop sign), signaling the entrance to a community that had always been oriented around the water side of homes. But Hunts Point Park was south of that entrance, with no waterfront, and filling in an area that had been forested and acted as a buffer between

HUNTS POINT PARK ADDITION

PORTIONS OF GOV'T LOT 3 SEC. 24 TWP 25 NR 4 E.W.M.

Sept 1951   Scale • 1" • 100'   Continental Eng. Co.

The Hunts Point Park Addition brought formal platting to an area that had evolved organically over the decades. Courtesy of King County Road Services Division.

Hunts Point and the adjacent agricultural and commercial areas. This change was so startling that residents of Hunts Point Park were given separate voting status at the Improvement Club during the incorporation process: it was not clear that they were really part of Hunts Point.

The new subdivision was just the beginning, however. Even more change was on the way: incorporation and the SR 520 corridor.

Creating the Town of Hunts Point

Incorporation did not happen in a vacuum, but was part of the larger wave of city-making taking place across the region in the 1950s. Rapid growth had led to very real concerns about the quality of life and the ability of communities to control their futures. The only incorporated cities on the Eastside in 1950 were Kirkland, Houghton, Redmond, Issaquah, Bothell and Renton. The entire area from Houghton to Renton and east to Lake Sammamish was unincorporated King County. And prior to 1969 the county was run by just three commissioners so no community had any local representation in county decision-making. (One of the last three people to serve as a County Commissioner, before the current home rule charter took effect, was Hunts Point native John Spellman who later served as King County Executive and Governor.)

To be fair, the county had provided Hunts Point with ferry docks and roads, and had recognized Hunts Point's organic platting. But three major concerns led the residents of the points communities to believe that county government no longer could serve their interests: land use, other incorporations in the area, and the proposed new bridge.

Prior to 1950 the area to the south of the Boddy-Hindle Road (now NE 32nd Street) was unplatted and consisted of farms and open space. Many viewed the Hunts Point Park Addition of 1951 as the precursor to the larger scale platting of the whole area into subdivisions. Furthermore, the large lots on the Point itself would seem ripe for division as well. Early plats in Medina had consisted of lots in the range of 6,000 to 8,000 square feet, and lots in new subdivisions, based on post-war suburban standards, were typically 7,200 to 10,000 square feet. In the 1950s the county had no comprehensive land use plans, so it would have been quite easy for a Hunts Point property owner to subdivide a large parcel into new home sites and sell those sites to builders. Long lakefront parcels had been divided this way in Medina and Yarrow Point, and repeating such a pattern on Hunts Point would have totally changed the character of the community.

The pressures of post-war suburban growth were being felt across the Eastside, and in 1953 Bellevue was the first new city to emerge. The original city limits of Bellevue were far smaller than today, and the population of the new city was under 10,000 people. But Bellevue leaders clearly had their mind on further annexations, and communi-

This view from Evergreen Point, across Fairweather Bay, shows Hunts Point in 1954, just prior to incorporation. Courtesy of Washington State Archives.

ties near Lake Washington, with their healthy tax bases, were attractive targets. The first areas to eliminate the prospect of annexation to Bellevue were Clyde Hill, the least developed of the points areas, and Beaux Arts Village, both of which incorporated in 1954, just a year after Bellevue.

After Clyde Hill took the plunge, the rest of the points could no longer dither. Medina had active factions pushing both incorporation and annexation to Bellevue, and Yarrow Point residents were considering incorporation as well as annexation to Bellevue or Clyde Hill. But since Hunts Point did not touch Bellevue or Houghton (Houghton was a separate city at the time, and annexed to Kirkland in 1968) its fate would be wound up in the decisions of Medina and Yarrow Point. Hunts Point leaders discussed the possibility of incorporating right away with the understanding that they might dissolve their new city and annex to Bellevue should Medina and Yarrow Point choose annexation.

Looming over all these discussions was the prospect of a second bridge across Lake Washington that would connect to a new freeway cutting across the base of the points. The first bridge, across Mercer Island, had opened in 1940 and no one foresaw the impact it would have on post-war housing development. The bridge was filling rapidly with commuters from new Eastside neighborhoods and by the late 1940s discussions were already underway about building a second bridge. Those discussions bore a remarkable similarity to more recent debates about cross-lake corridors, raising options of a parallel bridge across Mercer Island, or a Sand Point-Kirkland route.

The decision process was not a linear or clean one, but the possibility of a Montlake-Evergreen Point route was in the mix early on. In July of 1954 Governor Arthur Langlie and Seattle Mayor Allan Pomeroy agreed to pursue the Montlake-Evergreen Point route, and Medina's first comprehensive plan, drawn up in 1956, shows the proposed route almost exactly as it was built. Although the final decision was still ahead, Hunts Point residents would have had ample warning about the route, and becoming an incorporated town would give them a say in the critical questions of on-ramps and off-ramps.

In a letter written to residents of Hunts Point in February, 1955, Sterling Stapp, President of the Hunts Point Improvement Club (and its first mayor) summed up the concerns of the Club: "With the rapid development of the entire east side area and the building of the new bridge approach on 28th Street, it is inevitable that encroachment by housing developments, business areas etc. will

HUNTS POINT IMPROVEMENT CLUB

February 9, 1955

Dear Neighbor:

The next regular meeting of the Hunts Point Improvement Club will be held in the St. Thomas Parish House on Monday evening, February 14, at 8:00 o'clock.

Your officers believe that the community is entering a most critical era. With the rapid development of the entire east side area and the building of the new bridge approach on 28th Street, it is inevitable that encroachment by housing developments, business areas, etc., will eventually destroy the charm and value of our property unless immediate steps are taken to prevent it.

Your officers have become very concerned regarding this matter and have made a study of actions which must be taken if we are to preserve our type of living. We urgently need the help and advice of every resident of the Hunts Point area.

Won't you please be present at the meeting and be prepared to give us all the assistance you can.

An interesting and informative program has been arranged and refreshments as usual will be served.

We cannot urge too strongly the attendance of every single member of our community at this important meeting.

Very truly yours,

Sterling J. Stapp, President
Hunts Point Improvement Club

Courtesy of Eastside Heritage Center.

eventually destroy the charm and value of our property unless immediate steps are taken to prevent it."

The process to get an incorporation measure on the ballot was fairly quick. The Hunts Point Improvement Club held a meeting on the topic of incorporation on February 15, 1955, at which citizens discussed an Improvement Club committee report that recommended incorporation over annexation. On April 14 the club brought matters to a head, with Mr. Stapp stating, with regard the proposed new bridge, "knowing what the future holds, we feel that the county government no longer fills our needs." P.B. Edes moved, and Lloyd Mousel seconded a motion that "we are in favor of incorporation as a fourth class town and that petitions be circulated and signed requesting the King County Commissioners to hold hearings and call for an election to determine the fact of incorporation as a fourth class town." The resolution was voted on separately by residents of Hunts Point itself, and residents of the Hunts Point Park subdivision. It passed 52 to 3 on the Point, and six to three in Hunts Point Park.

Volunteers quickly fanned out across the Point, and the incorporation committee submitted 93 valid signatures to the County Commission on April 24. Residents of Medina and Yarrow Point submitted signatures for incorporation at the same time.

After verifying the signatures of the three incorporation movements, the Commission held a public hearing on June 13 to discuss the boundaries of the proposed new City of Medina and Towns of Hunts Point and Yarrow Point. The Town of Clyde Hill had incorporated the year before, so one piece of the boundary was established, along Points Drive, east of Hunts Point Road. In the process of drawing up the rest of the boundaries Hunts Point managed to get all of the head of Fairweather bay within its borders, allowing creation of the Fairweather Yacht Basin which was already in the planning stages. Cozy Cove was split down the middle, with the property that would later become the Weatherill Nature Reserve split between Hunts Point and Yar-

When boundaries were finally set in 1955, the original Barnabee Park subdivision ended up straddling Hunts Point, Yarrow Point and Clyde Hill. Courtesy of King County Roads Division.

row Point. Although the future SR-520 corridor was already on maps, those drawing the boundaries did not foresee or did not care that parts of Hunts Point would be stranded and accessible only through Medina or Clyde Hill.

The form of government that Hunts Point could adopt was determined by state law: because Hunts Point would have fewer than 1,500 residents at the time of incorporation, it would be classified as a fourth-class "Town." This meant that it would have a directly-elected mayor who would be responsible for day-to-day running of the town, with the assistance of a Town Clerk. Clyde Hill had incorporated as a Town and Yarrow Point would also. Medina, with an initial population larger than 1,500, incorporated as a Third Class City, with a conventional council-manager form of government.

Once the boundaries and governmental forms were fixed, the County Commission accepted the petitions for all three areas and set one more hearing for July 5 and the vote for July 26. The ballot asked voters to approve the incorporations, and to select individuals for office should incorporation be approved. For Hunts Point, the offices would be Mayor, five town councilmembers, and town clerk-treasurer. Three individuals filed to be mayor, eight individuals files for the town council and one for clerk-treasurer. Voters could choose five council candidates and the top five vote-getters would form the council.

When the ballots were counted, incorporation was approved by a margin of 72 to 45. Sterling Stapp became mayor, receiving 69 votes. The five councilmembers receiving the most votes were: Gordon Anderson, Robert Bowden, William Madden, Chester Ries and James Warrack. Helen Buzard was elected town clerk-treasurer.

On the same day, Medina voters approved incorporation by a vote of 229 to 125, while Yarrow Point voters declined incorporation by a vote of 98 in favor and 110 against (Yarrow Point would successfully incorporate in 1959). Curiously, at the same time that incorporation supporters in Medina and Yarrow Point were moving toward the ballot, annexation movements in those communities were also gathering signatures. In the end, however, the incorporation vote passed before the annexation forces could get past the County Commission – sometimes

The home of Helen Buzard (nee Brewster) served for many years as the town hall, hosting council meetings and the Town Clerk's office. Courtesy of Washington State Archives.

timing is everything. (Annexation was not a popular idea in Hunts Point, since it did not touch Bellevue and the only annexation option in 1955 would have been Clyde Hill.)

As today, governing Hunts Point was a low key affair. The new council held meetings in various homes until the Town Hall was built in 1978. The first meeting was held in the home of Mayor Stapp. Subsequent meeting were held in home (and on one occasion, the garage) of W.G. Clark and later at the Buzard's home and various other homes after she moved.

The town's budget for 1957, the first full year of operation with a permanent staff and services, was $14,641. The largest line item was $2,872 for continued fire service by the existing Bellevue fire district. The King County Sheriff had agreed to continue to provide response service until the Town could get its own police protection, which it did in 1957, hiring Ken Day, who had been serving part time in Clyde Hill. The 1957 budget gave a generous $1,000 allotment to the Planning Commission for consulting services, and the Town's allocation of state fuel tax money gave it a street maintenance fund of $1,322. Salaries were modest, with Helen Buzard, the town clerk, receiving $600 per year, and Officer Day receiving $1,500 per year.

The main business before the new town, as is usually the case, was to

TOWN OF HUNTS POINT
BUDGET 1957

CURRENT EXPENSE

	Salary	Maintenance	Total
Mayor's Office		$ 150.00	$ 150.00
Clerk's Salary	$ 600.00		600.00
Clerk's Office		150.00	150.00
Insurance & Bonds		78.61	78.61
State Audit		200.00	200.00
Publishing, Printing Office Supplies		150.00	150.00
Legal Expense		600.00	600.00
Asso. Washington Cities		25.00	25.00
Registration & Elections		200.00	200.00
Planning Commission		1,000.00	1,000.00
Library (2mills on assessed valuation)		1,436.46	1,436.46
Police	1,500.00		1,500.00
Fire Protection (1mills on assessed valuation)		2,872.91	2,872.91
Police Judge		25.00	25.00
Social Securities Taxes		15.00	15.00
Reserve & Contingencies		4,315.89	4,315.89
Total Current Expense			13,318.87
STREET FUND			
Road & Street Repairs		1,322.41	1,322.41
Total Budget			14,641.28

The Town's 1957 budget fit neatly on one page. *Courtesy of Washington State Archives.*

gain firm control of land use. After all, the prospect of new subdivisions had been a primary impetus for incorporation, and the projects in question were still likely glimmers in the developer's eyes. The first development codes were approved by the Town Council on September 12, a mere six weeks after the incorporation vote. Ordinance No. 2 set lot sizes, No. 3 regulated structures, No. 4 prohibited commercial activities, No. 5 regulated waterfront structures and No. 6 regulated subdivision. The council then established a Planning Commission and charged it with developing the longer term vision for the town. The first formal development codes were written by Hunts Point resident and attorney John Erlichman, and remain largely unchanged today.

Within a short time another of the drivers of incorporation would rear its head: SR 520.

The Evergreen Point Bridge and SR-520

The Mercer Island bridge had opened in 1940 at the tail end of the Depression. Few homes were built during the Depression and World War II brought nearly all non-government development to a halt, so for a period of about 15 years, very little new housing or commercial space was built anywhere in the country. Then, in the years following

the War, the dam of demand burst, with newly employed G.I.s looking for homes for their expanding families. Between 1950 and 1960
the population of King County would increase by 200,000 people with
the majority of that growth taking place in the suburbs. Developers
began following the "Levittown" pattern, building brand new communities well outside established cities where farm and forest land was
inexpensive.

In the Seattle area this meant development to the north and south, in
areas such as Shoreline, and Burien. But before Interstate 5 was built,
these areas were not easily accessible and commutes were slow. That
sleek new bridge to the east, however, offered an easy commute to
Seattle from the pleasant and largely untouched lands of the Eastside.
And so the developers came, with firms like Bell and Valdez building
thousands of homes for commuters.

It was not long before the State Highway Department recognized
that the Mercer Island bridge would soon reach capacity, and that a
new bridge would be needed. The first study of the cross-lake corri-

*The SR 520 corridor cuts across the south part of Hunts Point. The interchange shown here is being
substantially rebuilt. Courtesy of Washington State Archives.*

dor, released in 1951 concluded that a new bridge was not needed yet, but would be soon. Governor Langlie liked the idea, however, and by 1952 the wheels were in motion. Arguments over the route continued for several years, with Seattle vehemently opposing a bridge through Montlake, but ultimately that route was chosen. (Not surprisingly, Montlake has proven to be the most problematic section of the 2012 expansion of SR 520.)

Once the Highway Department settled on the Montlake-Evergreen Point route for the new bridge, it needed to design the contours of the approach highway. As it turned out, most of the area selected for the new freeway was agricultural or undeveloped, and few residents lost their homes. The route slashed through the proposed new Fairweather Bay Yacht Basin development, but construction had not yet begun, so the developer rounded off the channel and left four lots stranded on the other side of the freeway. Hunts Point Park fell just outside of the right of way to the north and only got a small clip off its southwest corner.

Homes in the Fairweather Yacht Basin and Hunts Point Park neighborhoods are seen on the right, as the approaches to the Evergreen Point Bridge are cleared and graded. Courtesy of the Washington State Archives.

The larger question was where the on- and off-ramps would be located. 84th Avenue was the main arterial of the area, and it made sense to locate the ramps at the base of Hunts Point. Furthermore, Medina's 1956 comprehensive land use plan envisioned a commercial center where the Yabuki greenhouses stood and where Medina Circle is today, so ramps at 84th Avenue would have served that new center. In the end, negotiation among the four small cities and towns that intersect at that point resulted in the split ramp of today, with east-directed ramps at 92nd Avenue in Yarrow Point and west-directed ramps in Hunts Point.

In the political climate of the time, the Highway Department did not need to pay much attention to mitigating the impacts of a project like SR 520. Compensation for the violence done to wetlands and previously very peaceful neighborhoods was limited to some narrow paths (now the Loop Trail) and a pedestrian overpass to Three Points Elementary. The process at the time contrasts sharply with the extensive and very expensive mitigation provided to Mercer Island as part of the expanded Interstate 90 project in the 1980s and to the points communities as part of the SR 520 expansion underway as of this writing in 2011.

Disruptive as it was, the new corridor did cement the points communities' position as the most conveniently located residential area in the region. No area has shorter commutes to all of the major job centers and commercial and cultural amenities of the region. Hunts Point has managed to retain its sylvan flavor while, at the same time, being in the middle of a vibrant metropolitan area, and owes a debt for that status to the SR 520 corridor.

INCHING TOWARD THE 21ST CENTURY

Since incorporation, change has been slow on Hunts Point – exactly the way that residents prefer. Property on the Point was largely built out by the 1960s, and with the exception of the Hunts Point Lane development, completed in the late 1970s, there were few opportunities to alter the landscape after the SR 520 corridor was finished.

Hunts Point's elegant Town Hall reflects the natural, low key style of the community. Courtesy of the Town of Hunts Point.

Town Hall

For its first 23 years the Town Council met in private homes – after all, there were no public buildings in the town at all. Eventually the town decided to build a town hall. The remnants of the Bay School site that had not been in the path of SR 520 were still owned by the Bellevue School District, and Hunts Point acquired this property for a town hall and park.

Noted Northwest architect Omer Mithun was hired to design the new building, and it was financed with a local bond issue. To make things easy, one Hunts Point citizen, D.K. McDonald, purchased the entire bond issue, effectively loaning the city the money for the new town hall. The new hall opened in May, 1978, with dedication ceremonies taking place at the conclusion of Clean Up Day.

The Town Hall is an elegant but modest structure, in keeping with the minimalist governing approach of Hunts Point. The council chambers are scarcely larger than the living rooms that the council originally met in, and the building has only two offices for the town's part-time employees.

Wetherill Nature Preserve

The lowering of Lake Washington in 1917 created new wetlands at the heads of the three bays that define the points. All three of these fertile

Entrance to the Wetherill Nature Preserve, 16 acres of trees, wetlands and wildlife habitat. Photo by author.

areas had been farmed, but the unstable soils made them difficult sites for building houses. Fairweather Bay was dredged and filled to form the Fairweather Yacht Basin in the 1950s. Yarrow Bay was eyed for major development around that same time, but eventually saw development only on the southeast portion. Cozy Cove, however, remained largely untouched into the 1970s.

After the Hunts Point Lane development was completed in 1976, sixteen acres of land, with 525 feet of waterfront remained undeveloped. Of this, eleven acres were in Yarrow Point and five acres in Hunts Point. The majority of the waterfront was on the Hunts Point side of the line.

This much-sought-after property had been in the same family since Jacob Furth acquired it in the late 19th Century, likely from its original patentee, Neils Anderson. By the early 20th Century Furth had sold off all his holdings in the Points area, except this parcel, where he had built a summer home. Furth's two granddaughters, Sidonia and Mar-

The Wetherill Nature preserve features some of the last remaining untouched Lake Washington shoreline. Photo by author.

jorie Wetherill grew up romping through the property and swimming in the lake, and in the 1920s the property was bequeathed to them. Marjorie and her husband, Hugh Baird, moved into the old Furth family vacation house in 1942 and raised their family there, building a new home in 1971.

Not surprisingly, as the area filled in, land developers were eager to get their hands on one of the last pieces of undeveloped waterfront on Lake Washington. The sisters held out, and in 1988 Marjorie Wetherill Baird and Sidonia Wetherill Foley donated the entire parcel to the two towns with the stipulation that it always remain a publicly-assessable nature preserve. It is now the largest public open space in Hunts Point, and is managed by the Wetherill Nature Preserve Commission consisting of residents from Hunts Point and Yarrow Point and neighboring communities.

A CONSISTENT VISION

100 years ago Hunts Point began to solidify into a real community, with year-round residents, a school, community club and main street. This would soon be followed by a grocery store and the first Clean Up Day. Residents have always known they live in a privileged place and have worked hard to preserve the features that have made it so attractive.

When their underlying vision for the area was threatened by the post-war housing boom on the Eastside, Hunts Point residents supported incorporation and a strict zoning code that locked in large lots and the layout of the town. When the sylvan character of the Point was threatened, the town instituted a tree ordinance that has kept the town forested. When concerns about crime led to talk of gating the entrance, residents resisted that urge and opted for less intrusive ways to secure their properties.

A town strategic planning process in 2005 -- Vision 2006 -- carried these concerns forward. It emphasizes such key areas as security, tree preservation and lakeshore quality. And in typical Hunts Point fashion, the plan parcels out responsibility for the various elements to individual volunteer citizens. Hunts Point's vision, that has lasted for a century, is not just about what the town looks like, but what the residents do to keep it that way.

ENJOYING LIFE IN HUNTS POINT

THE LAKE

Hunts Point's attractiveness as a community derives in large part from the lake that mostly surrounds it. Lake Washington is among the finest urban water bodies in the world, large enough to remain clean and to accommodate large vessels, but small enough to allow commutes from all sides. In many ways, Lake Washington is the region's most important open space. Like a park, it provides relief from urban density and offers recreation opportunities to all.

For Hunts Point, Lake Washington evolved from the main mode of transportation to the principal amenity for most property owners. About two thirds of Hunts Point homes have waterfront, of which nearly all have docks and bulkheads that allow easy access to the lake. The lake provides excellent views and a sense of space and privacy. Unlike Medina, which had large waterfront estates from its earliest days, the Hunts Point community began as a series of vacation cottages owned by middle and upper middle-class residents of Seattle and then evolved into a commuter suburb. For many years the original cottages remained on the Point and provided a relatively affordable way for people to enjoy lakeside living. While nearly all of these cottages

Many Hunts Point residents enjoy lake access from their front lawns. Courtesy of the Washington State Archives.

have been replaced or extensively renovated, the lake remains central to life on the Point's waterfront.

For some residents the lake provides a restful view, but for many Hunts Point residents, the lake is a primary source of entertainment and exercise, especially in the summer. The water gets to a comfortable temperature by early summer, and the steady, but gentle slope of the bottom near the beach makes it ideal for swimming and water games. Fairweather Bay and Cozy Cove provide protected water for summer activities.

Long time residents, Fred and Alice Kimball organized sailing races on Cozy Cove. Children of the community learn how to sail and then competed for prizes awarded on Clean Up Day. The fleet began with the Kimball's boats, but families bought other small boats and the races ended up including dinghies from the Snowflake, Minto, Penguin and Sea Scouter classes. The Kimballs put on these races from 1961 to 1968, rain or shine, wind or no wind. They even organized a regatta that included guests from Canada.

But if the Kimball family was organizing the serene sport of sailing, the Deal family was taking the whole business of boating up a notch.

During the late 1920s at least three different people in the U.S. were busy inventing waterskiing, one of whom did it on Lake Washington. In the late 1920s, Don Ibsen, who later lived on the Medina side of Fairweather Bay, strapped boards on his feet and got tows around the lake until the new sport finally caught on. Ibsen was a tireless promoter and it did not take long for waterskiing to become immensely popular on Lake Washington and for inventive people to come up with new ways to entertain themselves behind fast boats. The Deals were among those adventurers.

Like many children growing up on the Point, John and Mick Deal occupied themselves by coming up with fun things to do on the lake. Their mother, Evelyn, is especially thankful for this because it's what inevitably kept them out of trouble. Many Hunts Point parents cite the lake as being a key feature for them because it gave their children something to entertain themselves with right in their backyard and kept them from searching elsewhere.

After the Deal boys and their friends grew tired of barefoot water-skiing, they decided to try something new to challenge their increasing water prowess. They built a water ski ramp in the middle of Cozy Cove which quickly became the center of all the local children's fun. The ramp slowly grew and about the time the boys were getting over 100 feet on the jumps, local neighborhood kids, Paul Wolcox and Dugal McKensy flew by on a hang glider.

"Jeff Joby originally bought two of them from some guys in Australia, who had the Regalia wing design worked out for using behind boats," recalls Mick Deal. They came around Cozy Cove about 15 feet above water using a ski rope. The boys were still somewhat out of control as they were still figuring out how to use their new toy. "So we dropped what we were doing on the ski jump and started flying with them," said Mick.

The Deal boys and their friends kept flying for about 4 or 5 years, refining the skill until it was perfected. Some of the boys had pilots for fathers and with their help they helped them figure out how to stay alive.

"We figured out that you needed a lot of room so if you got into trouble, like got into a stall you needed a lot of room so you could dive and come out," said Mick. "So we got longer lines and got up to a thousand feet to 14 hundred-foot lines. That saved us really."

"Kevin Coonic ended up in the trees." Mick laughed. "Everyone ended up in the trees, but nothing serious. Paul Wolcox, who ended up Mayor of Yarrow Point, crashed once."

Jeff Joby -- the kids called him "Joby Won Conoby," -- eventually went on to start a water ski company and was the first to take the gliders up to fly off a mountain. "He told [his friends] that it was an experimental tent." Mick laughed. "That's when all the fun began in the mountains."

While the Stimson family also delights in the typical spring and summer water activities, their favorite lake pastimes occurred in the winter. Conditions for such a treat have, however, been rare (occurring

On rare occasions the narrow parts of Fairweather Bay have frozen over, bringing skaters onto the lake. Courtesy of Town of Hunts Point.

in 1972 and 1978) since they've lived on Hunts Point.

"Twice since we've lived here it's been very very cold so the canals have frozen over," said Emily Stimson. The water was frozen just a few feet out beyond their wharf and was hard enough to skate on.

Bill and Emily Stimson kept their ice skates and decided to use them. It wasn't long before their neighbors like Bill Madden came out to watch. It was a very unusual sight. "Little kids came out and watched us," she said smiling. "It was quite a cold spell."

STAN SAYERS AND THE SLO MO SHUNS

Hydroplane racing is the perfect motorsport for the Puget Sound region. It takes place on water, rather than a racetrack, the powerplants were originally World War II Rolls Royce and Allison aircraft engines and the crews were full of Boeing airplane designers and mechanics. The sport is high risk and thrilling and is enjoyed from a beach or the fantail of a yacht, rather than from a hot grandstand. Hydroplane racing has always been a big deal on Lake Washington, and Seafair weekend is still the biggest event of the year.

And the sport has its spiritual home on the north tip of Hunts Point. Stan Sayers was a successful Chrysler dealer who had a keen interest in boat racing. He built his 7,000 square foot home, designed by noted Northwest architect Roland Terry, on the northern tip of Hunts Point in 1949, and built a special boathouse for his racing boats.

In his quest for the world water speed record, he commissioned Ted Jones, a Boeing engineer, to design a new hull that would skim over the water. Anchor Jensen, of the Jensen Motorboat Company, on Por-

Stan Sayers home on the tip of Hunts Point became the center of Northwest hydroplane racing. Courtesy of the Washington State Archives.

tage Bay, built the Slo-mo-shun IV, with all parts except the engine and propeller made locally. Early on the morning of June 26, 1950, Sayers left his Hunts Point boathouse and headed to a measured mile course off Sand Point, where he established a world record of 160.3 miles per hour. The design of the Slo-mo-shun became the standard for hydroplanes and a variation on that design is still used today, although the cranky surplus airplane engines have been replaced with smooth turbines.

In the years that followed, hydroplane racing became established on Lake Washington, with such early boats as the Miss Thriftway, the Miss Bardahl and the Hawaii Kai. The Sayers boats often won and had the advantage of a nearby boatyard – the Sayers boathouse. Instead of going to the pits near Seward Park, that would later bear his name, Sayers' drivers would head back to Hunts Point, and then return for the next heat under the Mercer Island Bridge hitting the starting line at full throttle.

SUMMER ON THE LAKE

From the beginning of community life on Hunts Point up to and during World War II, the isolation and limited population kept the residents sociable and bound together. The carefree days of summer inspired a perpetual mood of festivity and neighborliness. Few bothered to lock their doors and casual visiting among residents was almost expected. A favorite Sunday pastime was walking along a footpath that used to wind around the Point following the waterline. There are stories of canoe flotillas filled with festive residents singing songs in the bays.

An anticipated summer highlight was always the Fourth of July celebration held each year at Deercrossing, the clubhouse or sometimes on the Bilger property. People would gather for diving, swimming, canoeing and rowing competitions. Another common sport consisted of groups of men in canoes trying to upturn one another. The festivities would conclude with a family picnic and a dance in the evening. A long-time resident recalls the typical good times had on Hunts Point in a letter to a friend:

"It was a delightful time to remember—the Japanese lanterns, the dancing to music of a phonograph, the floating around in canoes in the summer evenings with two of the boys playing guitar and mandolin. The young people of now would consider it very tame, I'm afraid, but we loved it then."

"The Kucher's used to have a Fourth of July with fireworks down there," said long time resident Ned Brockenbrough, "but they moved and after that there wasn't any official Fourth of July activity but they decided in honor of the bicentennial in '76 we were going to have a really big deal and that began the big Yarrow Point – Hunts Point cooperation for Fourth of July." That celebration has continued ever since.

Spirited canoe battles were a favorite feature of summer activities on Hunts Point. Courtesy of the Town of Hunts Point.

Hunts Point youngsters show ribbons they won at the 1915 Fourth of July Celebration. Courtesy of the Town of Hunts Point.

Penny O'Byrne was one of the co-chairs, with Jean Brockenbrough for the first Fourth of July Celebration Hunts Point had with Yarrow Point. She remembers the extensive planning that used to go into the celebration. It used to start with a Spring Potluck, remembers Penny, to plan the events. One of the biggest hits the first year was a hot air balloon tethered to the land at 8592 Hunts Point Lane, before houses were developed there.

There were games for every age and also tug-of-wars. One year Michael Jackson, starting linebacker for the Seattle Seahawks, was there.

It was an unfair fight to say the least. A Treasure Hunt set up between the two points kept kids searching on their bikes for hours. Mike O'Byrne sat for two hours out in a boat on the lake waiting for kids to find the clue that led to him.

Girls ride in the back of a classic car during the 2007 Hunts Point-Yarrow Point Fourth of July Parade.

The Fourth of July Parade is all about participation, as both towns turn out to march down 92nd Avenue.

The Fourth of July Celebration still consists of five days packed with activities and events on Hunts and Yarrow points, with over 4,000 people showing up for the parade. The celebration starts with a kick off party, traditionally held on Hunts Point, and features the Fourth of July Grand Parade and a fireworks display over Cozy Cove. During the day participants enjoy hot dogs and strawberry shortcakes, a street dance with pizza, a pet parade, bingo and children's games.

OVERLAKE SERVICE LEAGUE

In addition to annual celebrations, residents also filled their time with more serious activities. After attending a meeting of the Seattle Fruit and Flower Mission, a public service organization, Mrs. Ida Curtis decided that Hunts Point should also form such a group. Her efforts resulted in formation of the Hunts Point Circle of the Fruit and Flower Mission in 1911. From this lone circle, the group grew to include circles in Bellevue, Yarrow Point, Evergreen Point and Medina. Eventually the women of Hunts Point agreed that there were enough needy people right in the "East-O-Lake" District to warrant breaking away from the Seattle organization and earning money solely for people in their own area.

The new organization was named the Overlake Service League. In order to aid poor families on the Eastside, this group organized a variety of projects to raise money. Throughout the years the Service League has held bake sales and rummage sales and has distributed milk, various baby items, clothes and some medical help to the needy. Once just a handful of women from Hunts Point, this organization now consists of ten circles throughout the Bellevue area with over 500 members administering to needy families.

In 2011, celebrating its 100th anniversary, the Overlake Service League announced a name change. Bellevue Lifespring "administers five youth and three education programs, and a range of emergency as-

Community service has always been an important part of life on Hunts Point, whether through the Overlake Service League or, as in this picture taken at Peggy Madden's home, the Red Cross. Courtesy of the Town of Hunts Point.

sistance to help struggling families and individuals with rent, utilities, food, clothing, daycare, car repair and more." The Overlake Service League is perhaps Hunts Point's most important legacy to the Eastside and exemplifies the spirit of community involvement that has defined the Point from the beginning.

THE GARDENING CLUB

With such beautiful lush gardens and environmentally minded residents, it's no surprise that Hunts Point has its own Garden Club. The Overlake Garden Club was founded January 12, 1939 to "increase the knowledge and love of gardening in its practical and artistic phas-

The Hunts Point Garden Club. Courtesy of the Town of Hunts Point.

es, to protect the native flowers, trees, and birds, and to stimulate community interest in beautifying neighboring property and highways."

Emily Stimson is currently part of the garden club with eight other women and explains how the meetings go. "We take turns giving the luncheon and then have a little program or speaker," she said, "or go to the Bellevue Botanical Gardens or another interesting garden." The club continues to meet and learn about the plants they love. They hope to continue doing so in the spirit of keeping Hunts Point beautiful.

Hunts Point has come a long way from its origins as a summer retreat for Seattle businesspeople, but some things remain constant: the lake, the trees and the sense of community. Those fortunate enough to live on Hunts Point waterfront can still orient their homes and much of their lives to the shore side as their forebears did over 125 years ago. Large yachts and floatplanes now tie up at docks where rowboats and small sailboat once did, and kids drive Jet Skis instead of paddling canoes. And all residents continue to enjoy life in a community that knows how to both celebrate and serve.

Fairweather Bay, 1941. Courtesy of the Washington State Archives.

ABOUT THE AUTHOR

Michael Luis is a third generation resident of Medina, Washington, and is author of a title on Medina in Arcadia Publishing's *Images of America* series. He lives with his family in the home on Evergreen Point Road originally owned by his grandparents, Medina pioneers William and Alma Park. Mr. Luis is a public affairs and communications consultant and was elected to the Medina City Council in 2011.